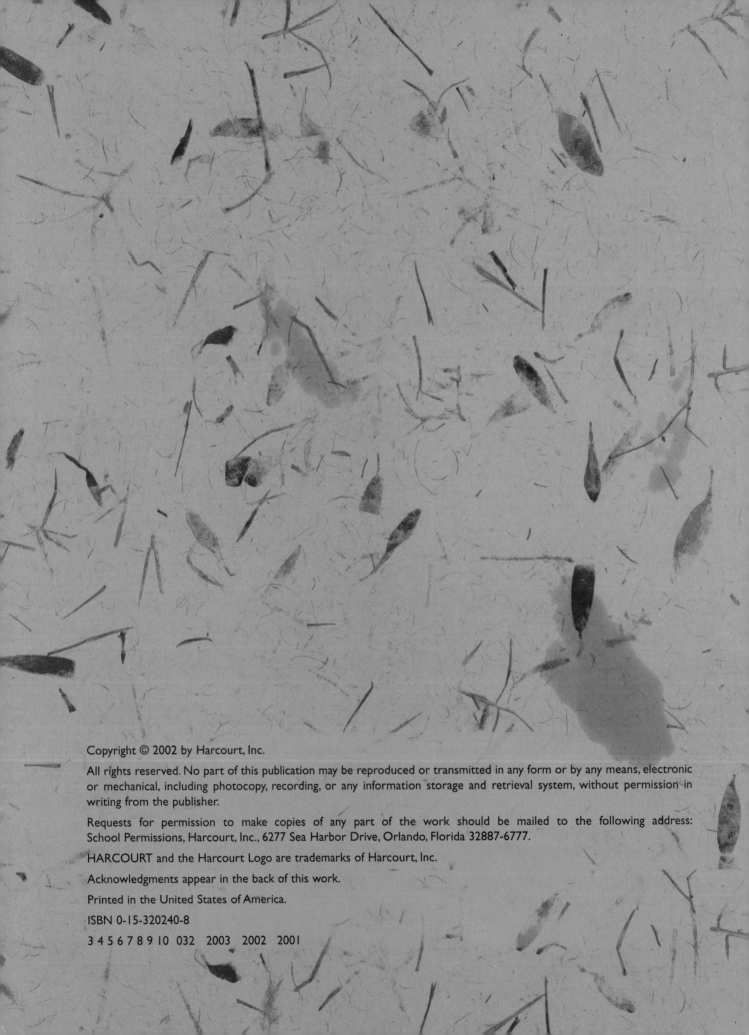

Requests for permission to make copies of any part of the work should be mailed to the following address: School Permissions, Harcourt, Inc., 6277 Sea Harbor Drive, Orlando, Florida 32887-6777.

HARCOURT and the Harcourt Logo are trademarks of Harcourt, Inc.

Acknowledgments appear in the back of this work.

Printed in the United States of America.

ISBN 0-15-320240-8

3 4 5 6 7 8 9 10 032 2003 2002 2001

Harcourt
Language

SENIOR AUTHORS
Roger C. Farr ◆ Dorothy S. Strickland

AUTHORS
Helen Brown ◆ Karen S. Kutiper ◆ Hallie Kay Yopp

SENIOR CONSULTANT
Asa G. Hilliard III

CONSULTANT
Diane L. Lowe

⧓Harcourt

Orlando   Boston   Dallas   Chicago   San Diego

Visit *The Learning Site!*
www.harcourtschool.com

Contents

Unit 2
Social Studies

Grammar • All About Nouns
Writing • Thank-You Note
• Friendly Letter   94

CHAPTER 11 Pronouns

CHAPTER 12 Writing a Friendly Letter

Unit 3 **Grammar • Verbs**
Writing • Dialogue
• Story   168

Science

Unit 4

Grammar • All About Adjectives
Writing • Poem
• Expository/Paragraph That Describes   **240**

Science

Math

CHAPTER 23   Adjectives That Compare

CHAPTER 24   Writing a Paragraph That Describes

Unit 5

Grammar • Writing • More About Verbs
• Directions
• Expository/How-to Paragraph   **316**

Fine Arts

Science

Unit 6 Grammar • Usage Wrap-Up
Writing • Book Report
• Expository/Research Report 388

CHAPTER 35 Troublesome Words

CHAPTER 36 Writing a Research Report

Handbook

Writing

Additional Writing Models

Writing Rubrics

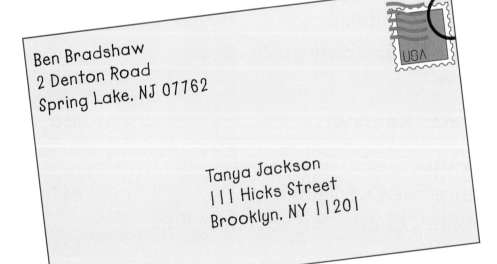

Ben Bradshaw
2 Denton Road
Spring Lake, NJ 07762

Tanya Jackson
111 Hicks Street
Brooklyn, NY 11201

Spelling

Handwriting Models

Thesaurus

Glossary

Vocabulary Power

Index

At a Glance

Listening and Speaking

Grammar, Usage, and Mechanics

Writing Forms

The Building Blocks of Language

The language that you read, speak, and write is made up of different parts that work together. Some of these parts you already know. Others you will learn about and use as you read this book. Which of these parts do you already know? Which parts help make up other parts?

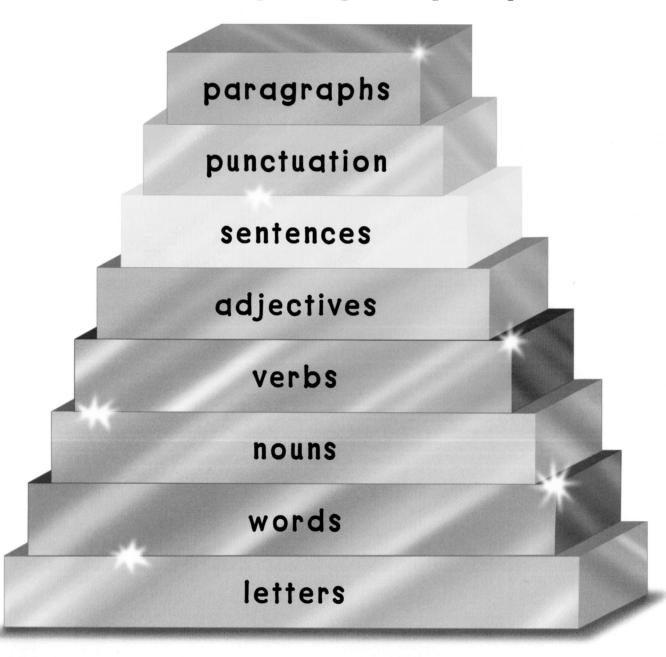

paragraphs

punctuation

sentences

adjectives

verbs

nouns

words

letters

The Writing Process

When you write, use a plan to help you. Think about *what* you want to write, for *whom* you are writing, and *why* you are writing. Then use these stages to help you. You can move back and forth between the stages of the writing process at any time.

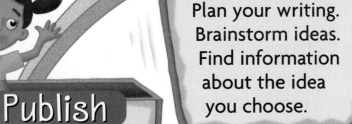

Prewrite
Plan your writing. Brainstorm ideas. Find information about the idea you choose.

Publish
Decide how you want to publish your writing. Share your writing with others.

Draft
Use your prewriting ideas to write a first draft. Do not worry about making mistakes.

Proofread
Check your writing for mistakes. Correct mistakes in capital letters, end marks, and spelling.

Revise
Read your first draft. Talk about it with others. Change parts to make your writing better.

STRATEGIES FOR WRITING

Use these strategies to help you write. Look for What Good Writers Do in every writing chapter.

What Good Writers Do

 List or draw your ideas before you write.

 Remember for whom you are writing and why.

 Use your own words.

 Use an order that makes sense.

 Use different kinds of sentences to make your writing interesting.

 Use exact words.

 Give examples.

 Revise your writing to make it better.

 Proofread for grammar, spelling, capitalization, and punctuation.

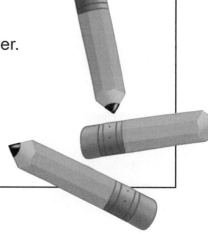

Keeping a Journal

Many writers keep a journal. A **journal** is a place to write down thoughts and record ideas for writing. A journal is also a good place to help you keep a record of interesting things that happen.

September 14
Ideas for writing

My favorite things
 −soccer
 −my fish tank
 −puzzles
 −visits from Grandma

September 15

Today I met Dana at school. Dana is from Laredo, Texas. She is good at drawing reptiles. She helped me draw a chameleon for my science project. I helped her with her spelling. We want to work together again soon!

Vocabulary Power

You may also want to keep a word bank of new words in your journal to use for writing. Look for a new Vocabulary Power word in every chapter of this book.

Keeping a Portfolio

A **portfolio** is a place such as a folder where you keep writing pieces, pictures, and other work. A portfolio helps you see how your work changes over time. Make a portfolio. Keep your work in it. Look at your work over time to see how it gets better.

Melissa's Writing Portfolio

21

Unit 1

Grammar
- All About Sentences

Writing
- Sentences About a Picture
- Personal Story

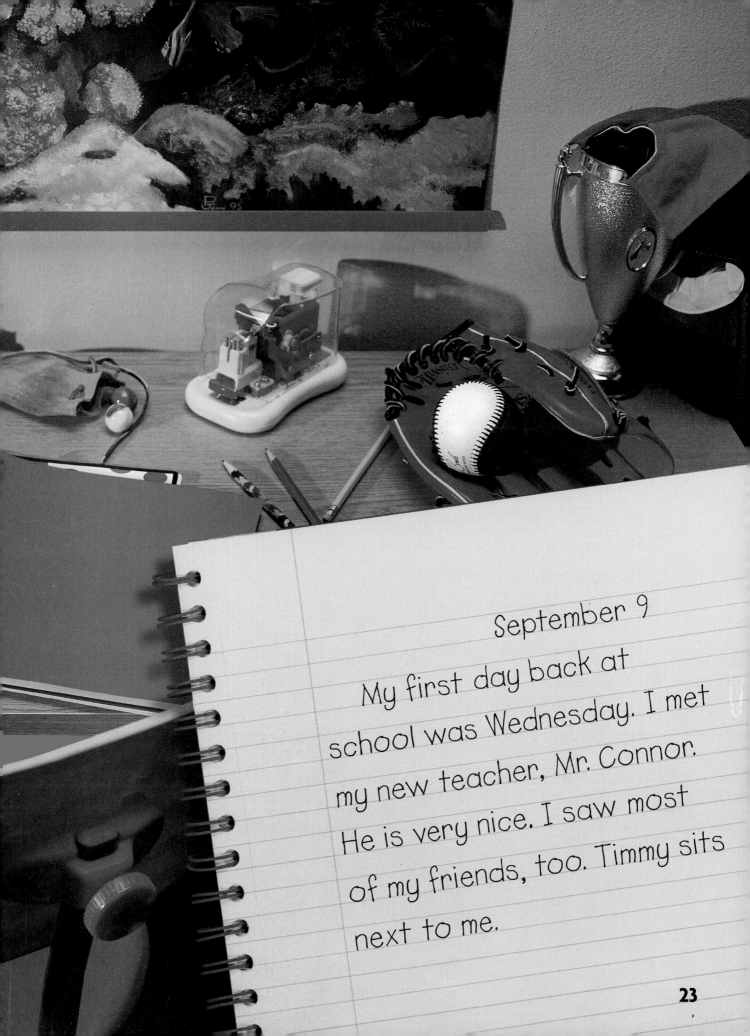

September 9

My first day back at school was Wednesday. I met my new teacher, Mr. Connor. He is very nice. I saw most of my friends, too. Timmy sits next to me.

What Is a Sentence?

Read the poem.

The Little Turtle

There was a little turtle.
He lived in a box.
He swam in a puddle.
He climbed on the rocks.

He snapped at a mosquito,
He snapped at a flea,
He snapped at a minnow.
And he snapped at me.

He caught the mosquito,
He caught the flea,
He caught the minnow.
But he didn't catch me.

Vachel Lindsay

Say clues for your classmates about an animal and what it does, but do not tell its name. Make your clues sound like the lines in "The Little Turtle."

> A **sentence** is a group of words that tells a complete thought. It begins with a capital letter and ends with an end mark.
>
> **T**he turtle swims in the pond**.**

Work with a partner. Add a word to each group of words to make a sentence.

There was a little _____.

He lived in a _____.

He _____ in a puddle.

He _____ on the rocks.

He caught a _____.

He _____ a flea.

He caught a _____.

But he didn't catch _____.

Word Order in a Sentence

The words in a sentence should be in an order that makes sense. If the words are mixed up, the sentence does not make sense.

Sentence   The boy plays a trumpet.
Not a Sentence   The plays trumpet boy a.

Guided Practice

Write each group of words in an order that makes sense.

1. Sol plays piano the.

2. Fern the beats drum loudly.

3. blows clearly horn He the.

4. Mona guitar the strums.

5. the Everyone to listens band.

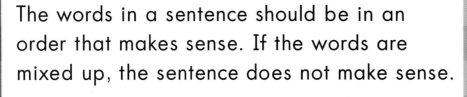

Independent Practice

Write each group of words in an order that makes sense.

6. Tony likes to hats wear.

7. are dresses pretty Purple.

8. Mary sneakers buys red.

9. Cara running has shoes.

10. wears José boots cowboy.

11. has Lucy pretty sweaters.

12. Pablo wear vests likes to.

13. Some baseball children collect caps.

14. wears Wally striped socks.

15. closet in Red the dresses hang.

Writing Complete Sentences What kinds of clothes do you like? Write sentences that tell about their color and style. Then draw pictures to go with the sentences. Put the sentences and the pictures together to make a catalog.

Beginning and Ending a Sentence

> A sentence begins with a capital letter and ends with an end mark.
>
> **J**immy likes to draw.
> **H**is sister likes to paint.

Guided Practice

Write each sentence correctly.

1. caleb mixes the paints

2. i always draw flowers

3. my mom likes to use crayons

4. dad enjoys cutting out pictures

5. my grandpa paints a picture

Independent Practice

Write each sentence correctly.

6. we can make a picture together

7. i want to draw the animals

8. you can draw the sky

9. megan can help

10. she is a good artist

11. we can cut out shapes

12. my little brother likes to use glue

13. he will glue the shapes

14. he can add glitter

15. we made a beautiful picture

Writing Connection

Proofreading Look through your Writing Portfolio. Choose a piece of writing. Check to see that each sentence begins with a capital letter and ends with an end mark. Fix any mistakes.

Hold down the **shift** key and press the letter key to make a capital letter.

Extra Practice

Write each group of words that is a sentence.

1. Steven is a fast reader.

2. He likes to read true stories.

3. The story he likes best

Write each group of words in an order that makes sense.

4. Lori good artist is a.

5. She also funny writes stories.

6. Many about animals are stories.

Write each sentence correctly. Use capital letters and end marks.

7. tami tells jokes

8. everyone laughs at her jokes

9. she likes to be silly

10. tami makes people smile

Language Play

Make a Sentence
- Take turns with a partner.
- Choose an item from each column.
- Put the words together and write a sentence.
- Score one point for each sentence.
- See who can get 5 points first.

the boy	has	a big sandwich
she	likes	very loudly
Jack	is	on the chalkboard
the girl	sings	a green sweater
the teacher	writes	always late

Writing Connection

Functional Writing: For Sale Sign Think about something you could sell. Make a sign that tells others about it. Write sentences for the sign. Use this sign as a model.

For Sale
I have a red bike for sale.
It costs only ten dollars.
Stop by if you want to see it.

Chapter Review

STANDARDIZED TEST PREP

Read each sentence. Is it written correctly? Choose the best answer.

1. brooke wants a cat

   a. Brooke wants a cat

   b. Brooke wants a cat.

   c. correct as is

2. tim has a big dog.

   a. Tim has a big dog.

   b. Tim has a big dog

   c. correct as is

3. The boy finds a turtle.

   a. The boy finds a turtle

   b. the boy finds a turtle

   c. correct as is

4. A black horse Zack has.

   a. Zack has a black horse.

   b. zack has a black horse.

   c. correct as is

5. My dad keeps bees

   a. my dad keeps bees.

   b. My dad keeps bees.

   c. correct as is

6. has two Tia rabbits

   a. tia has two rabbits.

   b. Tia has two rabbits.

   c. correct as is

7. Simone fish likes.

   a. simone likes fish

   b. Simone likes fish.

   c. correct as is

8. Lee has an ant farm.

   a. Lee has an ant farm

   b. Lee farm has an ant

   c. correct as is

Visit our website for more activities with sentences:

www.harcourtschool.com

▣ Study Skills ▣

Using the Parts of Your Book

Most books have special pages that give information about what is inside the book. There is a **table of contents** in the front of your book. It shows the chapters, or parts of the book. It shows the page number of the beginning of each chapter.

There is a **glossary** at the back of the book. It tells the meanings of important words in the book. It is like a dictionary. Your book also has a thesaurus in the back. A **thesaurus** gives synonyms for words. **Synonyms** are words that mean almost the same.

Practice

Use the example page to answer the questions.

1. What is the title of Chapter 2?

2. On what page does Chapter 1 begin?

3. How many chapters are in this table of contents?

Answer these questions.

4. Where is the glossary of a book?

5. What can you find in a thesaurus?

TABLE OF CONTENTS

What Are the Parts of a Sentence?

Read the poem.

April Rain Song

Let the rain kiss you.
Let the rain beat upon your head
   with silver liquid drops.
Let the rain sing you a lullaby.

The rain makes still pools
   on the sidewalk.
The rain makes running pools
   in the gutter.
The rain plays a little sleep-song
   on our roof at night—

And I love the rain.

Langston Hughes

Talk with a group about something you like. Use complete sentences to tell what it does and why you like it.

A sentence has two parts.

- The **naming part** names who or what the sentence is about.

    Felipe likes the rain.
    The rain makes pools on the ground.

- The **telling part** tells what someone or something is or does.

    The rain **falls from a silver sky.**
    Felipe **walks in the rain.**

Write a naming part to complete each sentence.

_____ plays in puddles.

_____ looks like silver.

_____ dances on the sidewalk.

Write a telling part to complete each sentence.

The rain _____.

The rain _____.

The rain _____.

Naming Parts and Telling Parts

In a sentence, the naming part works with the telling part to tell a complete thought.

naming part	telling part
Jeff	kicks the ball.
The ball	rolls into the goal.

Guided Practice

Write each sentence. Circle the naming part. Underline the telling part.

1. Jeff plays soccer.

2. Pat kicks the ball far.

3. The ball rolls across the grass.

4. Jeff joins a team.

5. The team wins many games.

Independent Practice

Write each sentence. Circle the naming part. Underline the telling part.

6. Jeff goes to the first practice.

7. Dave and Maria are on the team.

8. Dave runs and kicks well.

9. Maria stops the ball at the net.

10. Jeff worries about his playing.

11. The coach helps him.

12. Dave helps Jeff kick better.

13. Maria helps Jeff stop the ball.

14. Jeff practices every day.

15. Jeff plays better now.

Writing Connection

Revising Choose a piece of your writing. Make sure your sentences are complete thoughts. Find the naming part and the telling part in each sentence. Add words if you need to do so.

Use your computer to help you fix your sentences.

Combining Parts of Sentences

Sometimes the telling parts of two sentences are the same. You can join the two naming parts using **and**.

Girls enjoy reading books.
Boys enjoy reading books.
Girls **and** boys enjoy reading books.

Guided Practice

Use *and* to join each pair of sentences. Write the new sentence.

1. Danny liked books about sports.
   Clare liked books about sports.

2. Mom read the newspaper.
   My teacher read the newspaper.

3. Beth found animal books.
   Joey found animal books.

4. Trisha got pop-up books.
   Tony got pop-up books.

5. Pam waited in line.
   Luis waited in line.

Independent Practice

Use *and* to join each pair of sentences. Write the new sentence.

6. My friends read.
   I read.

7. Gina loved the new book.
   Linda loved the new book.

8. John couldn't find a book to buy.
   Eric couldn't find a book to buy.

9. Kim looked on the joke book shelf.
   Eric looked on the joke book shelf.

10. Shana wanted to buy magazines.
    Lin wanted to buy magazines.

)))) Writing Connection

Drafting Think about a fun place.
Write sentences about it, like these:

    Tina went to the park.
    Maria went to the park.
    Tina and Maria went to the park.

Share your sentences with a partner.

You can use your computer to write and join the sentences.

Extra Practice

Write a naming part for each sentence.

1. _____ calls upstairs.

2. _____ comes downstairs.

3. _____ sings "Happy Birthday."

4. _____ is surprised.

5. _____ remembers what day it is.

Write the telling part of each sentence.

6. The children go to a birthday party.

7. They eat birthday cake.

8. Everyone brings presents.

Use _and_ to join the naming parts from each sentence pair. Write the new sentence.

9. Grandma sang "Happy Birthday."
   Mom sang "Happy Birthday."

10. Jane played a game.
    Tommy played a game.

40

Heads or Tails?

- Take turns with a partner.
- Choose a sentence from a book.
- Flip a coin or two-sided chip. If it is heads, say the naming part. If it is tails, say the telling part.
- You get one point for each sentence part you say correctly. The first player with 10 points wins.

Writing Connection

Sentence About a Picture Draw a picture that shows something you and a friend like to do. Then write a sentence about it. Make sure that your name and your friend's name are both in the naming part. Use this picture and sentence as a model.

Dennis and Tommy ride bikes.

Chapter Review STANDARDIZED TEST PREP

Choose the answer that best tells about the underlined words.

1. <u>Some people</u> have brown hair.

   a. naming part

   b. telling part

   c. complete sentence

2. <u>My Uncle Bill combs his hair.</u>

   a. naming part

   b. telling part

   c. complete sentence

3. <u>Tony</u> reaches the tallest shelf in the classroom.

   a. naming part

   b. telling part

   c. complete sentence

4. Mr. Thomas <u>reaches the tallest shelf in the school.</u>

   a. naming part

   b. telling part

   c. complete sentence

5. <u>Connie runs the fastest.</u>

   a. naming part

   b. telling part

   c. complete sentence

6. Steve <u>wears blue sneakers.</u>

   a. naming part

   b. telling part

   c. complete sentence

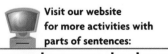 **Visit our website for more activities with parts of sentences:**

Study Skills

Using ABC Order

The letters of the alphabet are in a special order called **ABC order**, or alphabetical order.

a b c d e f g h i j k l m n o p q r s t u v w x y z

Words can be put in ABC order so that they are easier to find in long lists. Your book's glossary and thesaurus are in ABC order. Dictionaries are also in ABC order. Use the first letters of words to put them in ABC order. These words are in ABC order.

cook **f**riend **j**elly

When words begin with the same first letter, use the second letter to put them in ABC order.

d**a**rk d**i**sh d**o**g

Practice

Write the words in ABC order.

1. for, igloo, goat

2. meal, maybe, mother

3. star, sandwich, space

Answer these questions.

4. To find the word *sentence* in your glossary, would you look near the beginning, middle, or end?

5. On what page is *sentence* in your glossary?

Developing Ideas and Topics

Writers can find **topics**, or ideas, for writing in many ways. One way is to **brainstorm** ideas. When you brainstorm, you make a list of all the ideas that come to your mind. Then you can look at the list and choose the best topics for writing.

Read these sentences and look at the pictures about pets. How do you think the writers chose what to write about?

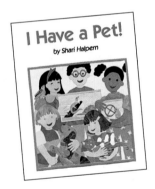

I Have a Pet!

by Shari Halpern

Sophie is my hamster. I give her food and water, and I clean out her cage. I take out the old, dirty wood chips and put in new, clean ones. Sophie likes to burrow under them and make a soft bed to sleep in.

This is my pet lizard. His name is Raymond. He lives in a glass cage with a rock and a branch that he likes to sit on. I make sure Raymond gets fresh water and crickets to eat.

Think About It

1. What were the most interesting things you learned about Sophie and Raymond?

2. Why do you think the two children wrote about their pets? How do they feel about their pets?

Writer's Craft

Developing Ideas and Topics

When you brainstorm, you think of many ideas for your writing before you start. Raymond's owner brainstormed this list of topics for his sentences.

Topics for Writing

My fishing trip

My pet lizard

My best friend

He chose to write about his pet lizard, Raymond. He thought that Raymond would be the most interesting topic. He also thought his classmates would like to know about Raymond.

Then he drew a picture of Raymond.

A. Brainstorm a list of ideas for writing about an animal. Then decide which idea would be the most interesting to you and your classmates. Use the Idea Bank if you need help getting started.

Idea Bank

What is my favorite animal?
  Where does the animal live?
  What color is it?
  Does the animal have fur?
What pet do I have?
  How do I help take care of it?
  What does it eat?

B. Draw a picture of your animal.

Writing and Thinking

Reflect Tell what helped you choose ideas from your brainstorming list. Write your ideas. Share your ideas in a small group.

Applying the Craft TAAS SKILL

Read these sentences about a picture that a student named John wrote. Think about the main idea of the picture and John's sentences.

main idea
sentence

I love to play checkers. My dad often plays with me. Sometimes I win!

Looking at the Model

1. What is the main idea of John's sentences?

2. How would John's writing have been different if he had not brainstormed ideas for writing or drawn a picture before he wrote sentences?

Your Turn

Draw a picture that tells about you and a pet or something you like to do. Then write sentences that tell about your picture.

Prewriting and Drafting

STEP 1 **Pick a topic.**

Brainstorm a list of ideas. Choose the most interesting idea. Circle it.

Things I Like to Do

1.

2.

3.

STEP 2 **Draw a picture.**

Your picture should show something about your topic. Add information you want your classmates to know.

STEP 3 **Write your sentences.**

Use your picture and What Good Writers Do to write a draft of your sentences. Make sure your first sentence tells the main idea of your picture.

What Good Writers Do

 Remember for whom you are writing.

 Don't worry about mistakes. You can fix them later.

Writer's Craft

Editing Your Sentences

Share your sentences about a picture with a few classmates. Together think about how you can make your sentences better. Use the checklist and the Editor's Marks to help you revise your sentences.

 My sentences tell about the main idea of my picture.

 Each sentence tells a complete thought.

Editor's Marks

∧	Add.
∧	Change.
ℯ	Take out.
≡	Use a capital letter.
⊙	Add a period.
⬭	Check the spelling.

Sharing with Others

Meet with a partner or in a small group. Show your picture. Read your sentences aloud.

●Handwriting●

Using Correct Position When Writing

Follow these tips for better writing.

Pencil Grip and Paper Position

✓ Hold your pencil and place your paper as shown.

right hand

Posture

✓ Sit up straight. Face your desk, and place both feet on the floor.

Stroke

✓ Make your letters smooth and even.

left hand

Pet
smooth and even

Pet
too shaky

Pet
too heavy

Pet
too light

Write these words. Follow the tips.

1. sentence

2. capital letter

3. end mark

Different Kinds of Sentences

Read the poem.

What Is Pink?

What is pink? A rose is pink
By the fountain's brink.

What is red? A poppy's red
In its barley bed.

What is blue? The sky is blue
Where the clouds float through.

What is white? A swan is white
Sailing in the light.

What is yellow? Pears are yellow,
Rich and ripe and mellow.

What is green? The grass is green,
With small flowers between.

What is violet? Clouds are violet
In the summer twilight.

What is orange? Why, an orange,
Just an orange!

Christina Rossetti

Talk with a partner about colors you like best and why. Then use a crayon to write sentences about your favorite color.

A **statement** is a sentence that tells something.

The apple is red.

A **question** is a sentence that asks something.

What else is red?

Write words to complete each question and statement. Add new lines to the poem.

What is white? A cloud is white.

What is yellow? _____ is yellow.

What is red? _____ is red.

What is _____? _____ is _____.

What is _____? _____ is _____.

Using Statements and Questions

A statement begins with a capital letter and ends with a **period (.)**.

José likes to swim**.**

A question begins with a capital letter and ends with a **question mark (?)**.

Do you like to swim, too**?**

Guided Practice

Write each sentence correctly.

1. the boys live by the beach

2. do they like to swim

3. they swim when the water is warm

4. can they swim far

5. they swim with their families

Independent Practice

Write each sentence correctly.

6. Zora swims well

7. when did she learn to swim

8. would you like to take lessons

9. you need a swimsuit

10. where can you get one

11. is Joe a good diver

12. Joe learned to dive last year

13. the girls swim very fast

14. did you see their flippers

15. flippers help them swim faster

Writing Connection

Asking Questions Write a question to ask classmates what sport they like best. Ask your question. Then write statements to tell their answers. Share your information with your classmates.

To type a question mark (?), hold down the **shift** key when you press .

Sentences That Go Together

Sentences that go together tell about one idea.

Jesse is a good swimmer. He can swim for a long time without getting tired. He can even do the backstroke.

A group of sentences that tells about one main idea is called a **paragraph**. The first line of a paragraph is indented, or written a little to the right.

Guided Practice

Write the paragraph. Leave out the sentence that does not belong.

1. The pool is fun. We float on our backs. We pet the pony at the zoo. The lifeguard shows us games. The fastest swimmers get prizes.

2. Which animals live in the water? Cats climb trees. Dolphins live in water but breathe air. Frogs need to stay wet. Turtles can swim well and spend part of the time in water.

Independent Practice

Write each paragraph. Leave out the one sentence that does not belong.

3.   What can we do at the beach? We can build sandcastles. Later, we can float on tubes. We can pick up shells, too. We can make snowballs.

4.   Fish make great pets. Goldfish are pretty and come in many colors. Dogs are fun pets. Most fish are quiet. Most fish don't eat much either.

5.   How do my friends learn to swim? Carla takes swim lessons. Ming practices every day at the pool. Roberto rides the bus to school. Alex uses a kickboard.

Writing Connection

Keeping to the Main Idea Read the paragraph. There is a line under the main idea. Write a sentence to add to the paragraph. Be sure it tells about the main idea.

Whales are interesting animals. They live in the ocean. They come up to breathe air. Whales have strong tails for swimming.

Extra Practice

Read the sentences. Write only the statements.

1. Can you jump off the diving board?

2. Mara likes to play tag.

3. Erik climbs the stairs to the slide.

4. Do you like the slide?

**Write each sentence correctly.
Use capital letters and end marks.**

5. the sand is not very hot

6. may I help make the castle

7. do you want the shovel

**Write the paragraph. Leave out
the sentence that does not belong.**

8.   The children worked together to make a sandcastle. Tasha put sand in a bucket. Then her sister added water. David did his homework. Kevin shaped the sand into a castle.

Language Play

Riddles

- **Take turns with a partner.**
- **Find an object in the room. Don't tell your partner what it is.**
- **Make up clues to help your partner guess the object. Use statements and questions.**
- **Write a few riddles like this one.**

> I am yellow. I am made out of wood. I get shorter each time I am used. What am I?
>
> A pencil

Writing Connection

Paragraph Remember that a **paragraph** is a group of sentences that tells about one main idea. One sentence tells the main idea. The other sentences are **details**. They tell more about the main idea.

> I like to go to Green Park with my family. — main idea
> We hike through the woods. We play on the swings or play tag in the big field. Then we usually fish in the lake and cook out. It's fun! — details

Write a paragraph about a place you like to visit.
Write a sentence to tell the main idea. Indent the first line.
Write detail sentences to tell why you like the place.

Chapter Review

Choose the answer that shows the statement or question written correctly.

1. We have jobs at home.

   a. we have jobs at home.

   b. We have jobs at home?

   c. correct as is

2. my sister clears the table

   a. My sister clears the table.

   b. My sister clears the table?

   c. correct as is

3. does Dad wash the dishes

   a. Does Dad wash the dishes.

   b. Does Dad wash the dishes?

   c. correct as is

4. Lee takes out the trash

   a. Lee takes out the trash?

   b. Lee takes out the trash.

   c. correct as is

Write the paragraph. Leave out the sentence that does not belong.

5.   I keep my room clean. I leave my socks on the floor. I put my toys away. I fold my shirts and make my bed.

Visit our website for more activities with statements and questions:
www.harcourtschool.com

■ Vocabulary ■

Homophones TAAS SKILL

> **Homophones** are words that sound alike but have different spellings and meanings. Knowing homophones and their meanings will help you spell words correctly.
>
> I **see** the boat on the **sea**.

Practice

Write the two words that sound alike in each pair of sentences. Tell how they are different.

1. Did you hear the news?

   The baseball player will be here soon.

2. I like to write stories.

   Do you want to read one right now?

3. Where are you going?

   Will you wear your new shoes?

4. Malik ate a plum.

   Yoko will eat eight grapes.

5. Maria won the race.

   Was she in one race or two?

More Kinds of Sentences

Read the poem.

Hurry!

Hurry! says the morning,
Don't be late for school!

Hurry! says the teacher,
Hand in papers now!

Hurry! says the mother,
Supper's getting cold!

Hurry! says the father,
Time to go to bed!

slowly, says the darkness,
you can talk to me . . .

Eve Merriam

What are some things you say when you are in a hurry? What do you say when you want someone to do something? Say them to a classmate. Act them out.

An **exclamation** is a sentence that shows strong feeling.

Bill's drawing is super! It is great!

A **command** is a sentence that tells someone to do something.

Show me the drawing. Please give it to me.

What do you think the two characters in the picture are saying? Write one exclamation and one command for each bubble.

63

Exclamations and Commands

An exclamation is a sentence that shows strong feeling. It ends with an **exclamation point (!)**.

Making salad is a great idea**!**

A command is an order. It usually ends with a **period (.)**.

Mix the fruit together**.**

Guided Practice

Write the exclamations and the commands. Use the correct end marks.

1. What a good cook Tom is

2. Get Tom's cookbook

3. Open the book, please

4. Turn to the first recipe

5. That fruit salad looks great

Independent Practice

Write the exclamations and the commands. Use the correct end marks.

6. I just love strawberries

7. Taste a cherry, Tracy

8. Get Ricardo a bowl of peaches

9. Do not give me any bananas

10. Cream with fruit is great

11. What a yummy treat this is

12. Cody, have some fresh fruit

13. Give Pat a spoon

14. Sit down and eat

15. What different tastes we all have

Writing Connection

Writing a Recipe Draw your favorite fruit. Write sentences that tell someone how to fix the fruit the way you like to eat it. Make each sentence a command.

To type an exclamation point hold down the shift key while you press the ! key.

Using Different Kinds of Sentences

There are four kinds of sentences. Using different kinds of sentences makes your writing more interesting.

Stan is a good catcher.	**statement**
Is Stan a good catcher?	**question**
What a good catcher he is!	**exclamation**
Catch the ball.	**command**

Guided Practice

Change each statement into the kind of sentence shown in ( ). Write the new sentence.

1. Molly can hit the ball hard. (question)

2. She has a great arm. (exclamation)

3. Tennis is her favorite sport. (question)

4. Can you ask Molly yourself? (command)

5. Molly won the game. (exclamation)

Use different kinds of sentences to make your writing more interesting.

Independent Practice

Change each statement into the kind of sentence shown in ( ). Write the new sentence.

6. The play starts at eight. (question)

7. Someone is in my seat. (question)

8. Should you ask her to move? (command)

9. Anna has the lead in the play. (question)

10. She is a good actress. (exclamation)

11. Do you want to look at the costumes? (command)

12. Teddy's mom made them. (question)

13. They are beautiful. (exclamation)

14. Do you want to listen to the band? (command)

15. The music is nice. (question)

Writing Connection

Revising Look through your Writing Portfolio. Choose one piece of writing. Look at the kinds of sentences you used. Could you change any sentences to different kinds of sentences? Revise your writing.

Use Editor's Marks to make changes. Then copy the changes onto the document on the computer.

Extra Practice

Write only the exclamations and the commands. Use the correct end marks.

1. What an exciting race
2. Who do you think is fastest
3. I don't know who will win
4. Get ready for the race to start
5. Watch Tama go
6. Look how fast Brian runs
7. Is that Wong in front
8. Wong is the winner

Change each statement into the kind of sentence shown in ( ). Write the new sentence.

9. We can find out who is tallest. (question)
10. Should you get a yardstick? (command)
11. Is it in the drawer? (statement)
12. You are really funny. (exclamation)
13. Kevin is the tallest. (question)
14. I think I am taller than he is. (question)
15. Will you measure Jeannie next? (command)

Language Play

Command Tic-Tac-Toe

- Take turns with a partner. You are X. Your partner is O.
- Pick a box. Use the word to give a command.
- If you give a command correctly, put a marker on the box.
- The first player to get three in a row wins.
- When you are finished, say an exclamation to show how you feel.

come	read	it
jump	talk	leave
throw	walk	run

Writing Connection

Directions Directions can help you find your way. Write directions that will help others find their way to your desk at school. Write each sentence as a command. Draw a map to explain the directions.

Directions to my desk

1. Walk to the row of desks next to the windows.
2. Turn left.
3. Stop at the last desk.

Chapter Review

Read each sentence. Choose the answer that shows it written correctly.

1. Let's write our own books.

   a. let's write our own books.

   b. Let's write our own books

   c. correct as is

2. How I love to draw

   a. How I love to draw!

   b. how I love to draw

   c. correct as is

3. Write the sentences here.

   a. Write the sentences here

   b. write the sentences here

   c. correct as is

4. What great pages these are

   a. what great pages these are

   b. What great pages these are!

   c. correct as is

5. Finish your work

   a. finish your work.

   b. Finish your work.

   c. correct as is

6. How well we work together

   a. How well we work together!

   b. how well we work together

   c. correct as is

Visit our website for more activities with exclamations and commands:

www.harcourtschool.com

◼ Technology ◼

Using a Computer

A computer can help you prewrite, write, revise, proofread, and publish your writing.

monitor —

CPU —

keyboard —

— printer

— mouse

A **word processing program** helps you write on your computer. The letters and words you write are called **text** . All the text in one piece of writing is called a **document** .

How to Type Text	Open a document. Press the keys on the keyboard.
How to Add Text	Move the cursor to where you want the new text. Type the text.

Practice

Type the riddle on your computer. Look at the Editor's Marks. Use your computer to make the changes.

What kind of fish can see at night (a starfish)
(you inserted above "can see"; ? inserted after "night")

In a personal story, a writer tells about something that happened in his or her life. As you read "Red Dancing Shoes," think about what happened to this girl and how she felt.

RED DANCING SHOES

by Denise Lewis Patrick   *paintings by James E. Ransome*

Grandmama went on a trip. When she came back, she brought everybody presents.

My present was the most special. It was a pair of the finest, reddest, shiniest shoes that anyone had ever seen.

"Thank you, Grandmama," I whispered.

"They're dancing shoes!" Grandmama told me. "Why don't you try them out?" she said.

Big Sister guessed just what I was thinking. "If you want to show off your shoes," she said, "come with me."

Big Sister walked out the door. I danced. Then I stopped and peeked down at my feet. My red dancing shoes smiled up at me!

"Can we stop at Nen's?" I asked. "I want to show her my dancing shoes."

Nen is Grandmama's sister. She's my favorite aunt. She always lets me swing in the big wooden swing on her front porch.

We turned the corner. I could see Nen sitting in her swing. I wanted her to see my red dancing shoes *now*. Suddenly those shoes started running. I was running too.

"Nen! Look!" I shouted.

"Be careful," Big Sister said.

Just as Nen looked up at me, I tripped on a rock. "WOOF!" I fell onto the dusty path, making a smoky brown cloud all around me.

Nen was off the swing in a second, picking me up.
Big Sister was dusting off my clothes. I looked down
at my feet. The beautiful, shiny, wonderful, red
dancing shoes were sticky and blotchy and muddy.

"M-My dancing shoes!" I cried. I couldn't
take my eyes off my shoes. They didn't
look new anymore. They didn't look
pretty anymore. I bet they
couldn't even dance anymore.

"Let's sit down," Nen said. She went inside and brought us glasses of cool lemonade. "Do you feel better?" she asked.

"No," I said.

"I see you have pretty new shoes," she said.

"Not anymore," I said.

"Those are her dancing shoes," said Big Sister.

"I can't dance in them now," I told Nen.

"Are you sure?" she asked me.

I turned my toes in. Then I turned my toes out. My littlest toes started feeling funny.

"It's not the same," I sighed. "They used to be shiny and red and new."

"Let's go into the kitchen," Nen said.

She took my hand and smiled her secret smile. Then she sat me on a chair and unbuckled my shoes. She took a cloth and ran some water over it.

Nen pulled one of my feet onto her lap. The she held the cloth tight and rubbed it back and forth over my shoe. She did the same thing to the other one.

"All right," she smiled. "How do you like your dancing shoes now?"

I looked. I blinked. I looked again.

"MY SHINY, RED DANCING SHOES ARE BACK!" I shouted. I jumped off the chair and danced the Twist.

"I love my clean, shiny, red dancing shoes," I giggled, spinning around and around.

Big Sister looked at Nen's big kitchen clock and said, "We'd better get on home."

This time, I walked—I did not run. I looked down at my shiny red dancing shoes. They smiled at me ... again.

Think About It

1. Who is telling the story about the red dancing shoes? How do you know?

2. How does the girl feel when she first gets her new shoes? How does she feel when she thinks they are ruined?

Parts of a Personal Story

In "Red Dancing Shoes," the writer tells about something special that happened to her. Because she is telling about herself, she uses words such as *I*, *me*, and *my* in her story. She also uses time-order words, such as *then* and *now*, to show the order in which things happened.

On a sheet of paper, complete the sequence chart for "Red Dancing Shoes."

First

What is this personal story about?
What happened?

Next

What happened next?

Last

What happened at the end?

A Student Model

TAAS SKILL

Cara liked reading about what happened to the girl with the red shoes. She wrote a story about what happened when she got glasses. Read her story and think about what happens.

My Purple Glasses

This year when I started school, I could not read the board well. The words looked fuzzy. I told my mom about this. She thought I might need glasses. I was upset. How would I look in glasses?

Soon my mom took me to the eye doctor. First I tried on some big glasses. They looked bad. Then I found some purple glasses. I liked them. The next week I wore my glasses to school. Everyone said I looked cool! In class, I could read all the words on the board, too.

A good beginning helps get readers interested.

Time-order words help show the order in which things happen.

Looking at the Model

1. Who tells the story? How do you know?

2. What is the story about?

3. What happens first? What happens next?

4. How does Cara feel at the end? Why?

Writer's Craft

Find the different kinds of sentences Cara used in her story. How do they help make the story better?

Time-Order Words

Cara used the words *this year*, *soon*, *first*, *then*, and *the next week*. How do they help you know the order in which things happened?

Prewriting

Before Cara wrote her personal story, she drew pictures and made a list of ideas for her story. Then Cara thought about her classmates who would read her story. She thought they would like to hear about the time she got glasses.

Cara used this sequence chart to write the events in the order they happened.

First

What is this personal story about? What happened?
This year I could not read the board well. My mom took me to the eye doctor for glasses.

Next

What happened next?
I didn't want any of the glasses. I thought they would look bad.

Last

What happened at the end?
I found some purple glasses. I wore them to school. Everyone said I looked cool. I could see well.

Your Turn

STEP 1 **Think of ideas.**

Make a list of things that have happened to you. Draw or write your ideas.

STEP 2 **Choose an idea.**

Think about who will read your personal story. Choose an idea that you and your readers will like.

STEP 3 **Complete a plan.**

List the events in the order they happened.

First

What is this personal story about?
What happened?

Next

What happened next?

Last

What happened at the end?

Drafting

Cara used her sequence chart to write a draft of her personal story on her computer. She worked quickly because she knew a draft is just a first try. She did not worry about making mistakes. She knew she could fix them later.

DRAFT My Purple Glasses

This year when I started school, I could not read the board well. The words looked bad and fuzzy. I told my mom about this. She thought I might need glasses. I was upset.

Soon my mom took me to the eye doctor. First I tried on some big glasses. They looked bad. I found some purple glasses. I liked them. I wore my glasses to school. Everyone said I looked cool!

Read Cara's first draft. See how it follows her sequence chart. What might she write next?

First

What is this personal story about? What happened?

This year I could not read the board well. My mom took me to the eye doctor for glasses.

Next

What happened next?

I didn't want any of the glasses. I thought they would look bad.

Last

What happened at the end?

I found some purple glasses. I wore them to school. Everyone said I looked cool. I could see well.

- ☑ Remember why you are writing and who will read your personal story.
- ☑ Be sure all your sentences tell about your personal story.
- ☑ Tell what happened in order.
- ☑ Use different kinds of sentences.

Your Turn

Use your sequence chart and What Good Writers Do to write a draft of your personal story.

You can write your draft quickly on a computer.

Revising

Cara shared her draft with some classmates. They had some ideas about how to make it better. Read to see how Cara **revised** her personal story.

 DRAFT

My Purple Glasses

This year when I started school, I could not read the board well. The words looked ~~bad and~~ fuzzy. I told my mom about this. She thought I might need glasses. I was upset. ∧ How would I look with glasses?

Soon my mom took me to the eye doctor. First I tried on some big glasses. They looked bad. ∧ Then I found some purple glasses. I liked them. ∧ The next week I wore my glasses to school. Everyone said I looked cool! In class, i could read all the words on the bord, too

Your Turn

Now share your personal story with some partners. Ask them how to make it better. Use What Good Writers Do and the Editor's Marks to make changes.

Proofreading

Cara read her story one more time. She looked for mistakes. Think about why she made the changes in red.

DRAFT My Purple Glasses

This year when I started school, I could not read the board well. The words looked ~~bad and~~ fuzzy. I told my mom about this. She thought I might need glasses. I was upset. ∧ How would I look with glasses?

Soon my mom took me to the eye doctor. First I tried on some big glasses. They looked bad. ∧Then I found some purple glasses. I liked them. ∧The next week I wore my glasses to school. Everyone said I looked cool! In class, i could read all the words on the ⌒bord, too⊙
                                        board

What Good Writers Do

✔ Make sure each sentence begins with a capital letter.

✔ Be sure each kind of sentence has the correct end mark.

✔ Check your spelling.

Editor's Marks

= Use a capital letter.

⊙ Add a period.

◯ Check the spelling.

Your Turn

Read your personal story again. Use What Good Writers Do and the Editor's Marks to fix any mistakes.

You can add new sentences on a computer without rewriting the story.

Publishing

Cara copied some photos of herself. Then she cut them out and glued them onto a copy of her personal story to share with her friends.

Your Turn

Make a clean copy of your story. You can use your computer, if you like. Here are some other ideas for publishing your story in a special way.

- **Turn your story into a comic strip.**
  Draw pictures to show the beginning, the middle, and the end of your personal story. Add speech bubbles to show what different people say in each part of the story.

- **Make a flip book.**
  Draw a picture for each event. Attach the flip book to a clean copy of your story.

Add your finished personal story to your Writing Portfolio.

Listening and Speaking

Sharing Your Writing

You can share something that happened to you by reading your personal story aloud. Think about how to keep your listeners' interest. Practice these tips.

Speaking Tips

- Hold your paper low. This way your listeners can see your face and hear you better.
- Use your voice to show funny, sad, or exciting parts of your story.
- Your listeners should be able to hear statements, questions, commands, and exclamations by the way you use your voice.
- Speak loudly and clearly enough to be heard.

Listening Tips

- Listen to find out what event the person is telling about. What is the story's main idea?
- What happens first, next, and last?
- How does the story end? Does the ending surprise you?

What Is a Sentence? pages 24–25
Write each group of words that is a sentence.

1. School starts today.
2. gets up early
3. Mai eats breakfast.
4. the school bus

Word Order in a Sentence pages 26–27
Write each group of words in an order that makes sense.

5. Lee ahead of us runs.
6. Amy with me walks.
7. to us waves Sal.
8. the bus Max sees.

Beginning and Ending a Sentence pages 28–29
Write each sentence correctly.

9. the bus stops here
10. we get in a line

Naming Parts and Telling Parts pages 36–37
Write each sentence. Circle the naming part. Underline the telling part.

11. Tomas gets on the bus.
12. He helps his friend.
13. Sue and Mai sit together.
14. Our driver shuts the door.

Combining Parts of Sentences pages 38–39
Use *and* to join each pair of sentences. Write the new sentence.

15. Todd sat behind us.
    Sam sat behind us.
16. Amy talked.
    I talked.
17. Matt waved.
    Jim waved.

Using Statements and Questions pages 54–55
Write each sentence correctly.

18. what is your name   **19.** you can sit with us

20. are you in second grade   **21.** we just moved here

Sentences That Go Together pages 56–57
Write the paragraph. Leave out the sentence that does not belong.

22.   I really like my new school. Most of the kids are friendly. My teacher is so nice. I get to use a computer every day too. I like baseball.

Exclamations and Commands pages 64–65
Write each sentence correctly.

23. computers are great   **24.** Look at this game

25. teach us how to play   **26.** what fun this game is

Using Different Kinds of Sentences pages 66–67
Change each sentence into the kind of sentence shown in ( ). Write the new sentence.

27. You eat lunch at noon. (question)

28. You should get in line. (command)

29. This is the cafeteria. (question)

30. You should try this soup. (command)

31. Watch out for the desserts. (exclamation)

32. Are the peaches and plums delicious? (statement)

Social Studies

Who's Who

A Who's Who is a book that tells who people are and what they do. Work together with classmates to make a School Who's Who.

Make a Plan

- List the people who will be in your book. Include your classmates, your teacher, and school workers.

- Decide what you want to find out about each person. Make a list of questions to ask.

- Decide who will talk to each person. Decide who will write and draw each book page.

Get and Record Information

- Talk to the people. Ask them your questions. Write or tape-record the answers.

- Invite the people to speak to the class. Take notes. Videotape the speaker, if you can.

- Draw pictures of the people. Show what they like to do or how they do their jobs. If you have a camera, take photos, too.

Put the Information Together

- Use your notes to write a few sentences about each person. Use your computer if you want.

- Add your pictures and photos.

Publishing

- Make a clean copy of each page.

- Put all the pages and pictures together into a book.

- Ask your teacher to help you make copies of your book. Make one for everybody in the book and everybody who helped make it.

- Share your book. Take turns reading pages from it to the class or to other classes.

- Put your Who's Who on your school's website.

Books to Read

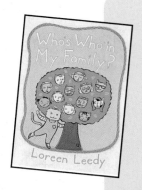

Who's Who in My Family?
by Loreen Leedy
Nonfiction
Students in Ms. Fox's class learn where they fit in their family trees. See how every family is special.
Award-Winning Author

Wilson Sat Alone
by Debra Hess
Realistic Fiction
A new girl in the class helps Wilson find out who's who at school.

Unit 2

Grammar
- All About Nouns

Writing
- Thank-You Note
- Friendly Letter

Nove

THANK YOU

Dear Vicky,
Thank you for the great pie you and your mother made for my family. It made our Thanksgiving dinner extra special! We are glad to have such nice new neighbors.

Your friend,

Ying

What Is a Noun?

Read the poem.

The Swing

How do you like to go up in a swing,
   Up in the air so blue?
Oh, I do think it the pleasantest thing
   Ever a child can do!
Up in the air and over the wall,
   Till I can see so wide,
Rivers and trees and cattle and all
   Over the countryside —
Till I look down on the garden green,
   Down on the roof so brown —
Up in the air I go flying again,
   Up in the air and down!

        Robert Louis Stevenson

What things does the person in the poem see while swinging? What things do you see when you swing? Make a list.

Naming words name people, places, animals, or things. A naming word is also called a **noun**.

My **brother** likes the **playground**.

Sometimes he sees **squirrels** there.

He likes to go on the **swings**.

Add new lines to the poem. Write nouns to complete the sentence.

Up in the air and over the wall,

Till I can see so wide,

_____ and _____ and _____ and _____

Over the countryside.

97

Nouns for People, Places, Animals, and Things

A noun can name a person, a place, an animal, or a thing.

My **uncle** is moving.
He is going to a new **town**.
He will buy a **dog** when he gets there.
He will need a **truck**.

Guided Practice

Choose a noun from the chart to finish each sentence. Use the clue in ( ).

People	Places	Animals	Things
aunt	house	dog	boxes
brother	park	cat	books

1. My _____ is moving. (person)

2. She packs many _____. (things)

3. I help carry out her _____. (animal)

4. I like her new _____. (place)

5. It is next to the _____. (place)

Independent Practice

Choose a noun from the chart to finish each sentence. Use the clue in ( ).

People	Places	Animals	Things
movers	kitchen	parrot	books
brother	dining room	dog	dishes
aunt	bedroom	squirrel	pans

6. The _____ are here. (people)

7. They unpack the _____. (things)

8. My _____ unpacks them, too. (person)

9. I take the _____ out of a box. (things)

10. I put them in the _____. (place)

11. Next door, a _____ barks. (animal)

12. I look out a window and see a _____. (animal)

Writing Connection

Diary Entry Think about what you did yesterday. Write sentences to tell about the people, places, animals, and things you saw.

Use **Search** and **Find** to find a word on your computer quickly.

Using Possessive Nouns

A **possessive noun** shows ownership. It tells what someone or something owns or has.

the **cat's** dish   my **dad's** hat

Add an **apostrophe (')** and the letter **s** to show ownership by one person or thing.

The truck of my uncle is red.
My **uncle's** truck is red.

Guided Practice

Use 's to rewrite the underlined words in each sentence.

1. The garden of my aunt is big.

2. The friend of my brother is working in it.

3. The friend of my sister helps, too.

4. The chair of my uncle should be put away.

5. The toy of the dog is on the grass.

> **Remember** Add an *apostrophe (')* and the letter *s* after a noun to show ownership.

Independent Practice

Use *'s* to rewrite the underlined words in each sentence.

6. Tom fixes <u>the fence of the neighbor</u>.

7. My brother trims <u>the rose bushes of my cousin</u>.

8. Leaves fall in <u>the hair of my brother</u>.

9. <u>The sister of Diego</u> brings us lemonade.

10. We all drink <u>the lemonade of Nina</u>.

11. A <u>nest of a bird</u> is on the ground.

12. I put it back in <u>the branches of the oak tree</u>.

13. Later Pam cleans <u>the rake of her father</u>.

14. Dave and I put away <u>tools of my aunt</u>.

15. <u>The neighbor of my aunt</u> asks us to work in her garden.

Writing Connection

Adding Possessive Nouns Look over a piece of writing in your Writing Portfolio. Find places where you could add possessive nouns to show what someone or something owns. Then check to be sure you used *'s* correctly.

To add an apostrophe ('), press ![key]. Do not add a space between the apostrophe and the next letter.

Extra Practice

Write the noun in each sentence.

1. My family likes to work hard.

2. We rake leaves.

3. Will we clean the house?

4. Soon we will work in the garden.

Choose the best noun from the box to complete each sentence.

ladder	shed	bush	brother

5. My dad trims the big rose _____.

6. Be careful on that high _____!

7. Please get the rake from the _____.

8. My _____ plants some flowers.

Rewrite each sentence. Use 's to rewrite the underlined words.

9. Hang on to the <u>leash of the dog</u>.

10. We do not want him to play in <u>the flowers of my brother</u>.

Language Play

I'm Going on a Trip
Play this game with a group.
- The first player begins by saying, "I'm going on a trip and bringing an _____." He or she adds a noun that begins with the letter *A*.
- The second player repeats what the first player said. Then he or she adds a noun that begins with the letter *B*.
- Play goes on in the same way through the alphabet. See how long your list can get!

Writing Connection

Functional Writing: Labels A label can show who owns something. Make labels for your things. Write them on self-stick notes if you want to do so. Then stick them onto your things.

Chapter Review

**Choose the best answer for each
underlined word or words.**

1. The <u>girl's</u> dog was lost.

   a. person

   b. place

   c. thing

   d. possessive noun

2. The <u>neighbors</u> helped her.

   a. people

   b. place

   c. thing

   d. possessive noun

3. Mrs. Jackson looked
in the <u>park</u>.

   a. person

   b. place

   c. thing

   d. possessive noun

4. Mr. Gomez found
the <u>dog's</u> toy.

   a. person

   b. place

   c. thing

   d. possessive noun

5. A little <u>boy</u> found the dog.

   a. person

   b. place

   c. thing

   d. possessive noun

6. The dog was in the <u>yard</u>.

   a. person

   b. place

   c. thing

   d. possessive noun

Visit our website for more
activities with possessives:
www.harcourtschool.com

▪ Vocabulary ▪

Compound Nouns

> A **compound noun** is made up of two nouns. The two nouns together make a new noun.
>
> gold + fish = goldfish
> base + ball = baseball

Practice

Look at each picture. Put together one word from each box to write a compound noun that names the picture.

door	dog	suit
star	foot	grass

house	ball	fish
case	hopper	bell

1.

2.

3.

4.

5.

6.

Nouns That Name More Than One

Read the poem.

Little Silk Worms

Little silk worms, if you please,
Eat up all the mulberry leaves.
Make cocoons as white as milk,
And we'll make clothes of purest silk.

Demi

Read the poem again with a partner. Tell in your own words what the silk worms are doing. Then talk about what is happening in the other pictures.

Some nouns name more than one.

Little silk **worms** make **cocoons**.

In a small group, play a game using nouns that name more than one.

- The first player says, "On my trip, I saw one (<u>noun</u>)."

- The next player repeats the sentence and then adds words to tell about two people or things.

- Keep going until each player has had a few turns.

- How many things did your group see?

Making Nouns Plural

Some nouns name more than one. Add **s** to most nouns to name more than one.

Tim received two **gifts**.

Add **es** if the noun ends with **s**, **ch**, **sh**, or **x** to name more than one.

Sue has three **dresses**.

Guided Practice

Write the correct noun in ( ) to finish each sentence.

1. On our class trip, I had lunch with my two (friends, friendes).

2. First we sat on three (chairs, chaires).

3. We put three (sandwichs, sandwiches) on the picnic table.

4. We also got out three (pears, peares).

5. Then we shared our three (lunchs, lunches).

Independent Practice

Write the correct noun in ( ) to finish each sentence.

6. My class went on a trip with two other (classs, classes).

7. We took two (buss, buses) to get to the park.

8. There we met with three park (rangers, rangeres).

9. They showed us many different (plants, plantes).

10. They told us about the (animals, animales).

11. We saw something move in the (bushs, bushes).

12. It was a family of (foxs, foxes).

13. At lunchtime we sat on (benchs, benches) to eat.

14. We shared our bread with some (birds, birdes).

15. After lunch we planted (flowers, floweres).

Writing Connection

Revising Look through your Writing Portfolio. Choose one piece of writing. Find nouns that name more than one. Check to see if you added *s* or *es* correctly. Revise your writing.

Use a computer to revise. Place the cursor at the end of the word. Type the letters you need to add.

Plural Nouns That Change Spelling

Some nouns change spelling to name more than one.

One	More Than One	One	More Than One
child	→ children	foot	→ feet
man	→ men	tooth	→ teeth
woman	→ women	mouse	→ mice
wife	→ wives	wolf	→ wolves

Guided Practice

Write the noun in ( ) to mean more than one.

1. Evan brought two pictures of (mouse) to class.

2. Latasha showed a painting of three (wolf).

3. Antonio shared a book about many famous (man) and (woman).

4. Holly showed two (leaf) that she found on a class trip to the park.

5. All the (child) enjoyed this show-and-tell day.

Remember Some nouns change spelling to name more than one.

Independent Practice

Write the noun in ( ) to mean more than one.

6. Mrs. Min took the (child) to the zoo.

7. Two (man) passed out maps.

8. Their (wife) were the tour guides.

9. The (woman) took the class to see the lions.

10. Jasmine liked watching all the (wolf).

11. The gorilla scratched his ears with both his (foot).

12. The guides showed them some special (mouse).

13. The biggest mouse had very large (tooth).

14. The class thanked the two (woman) for the tour.

15. All the (child) had a good time.

Writing Connection

Giving Reasons Think about a trip you have taken and what you liked about it. Then write a paragraph to tell friends why they should take the trip, too. Include plural nouns as you tell about details you think others would like.

Use a computer to write your paragraph. Save your writing. Add more details later.

Extra Practice

Write the noun in ( ) to mean more than one.

1. Barry, Carlos, and their class slept under the (star).

2. They slept in sleeping (bag).

3. They told each other silly (joke).

4. The next day they made (sandwich) for lunch.

5. They also ate ripe (peach).

6. After lunch the class washed their (dish).

7. That was when Carlos broke two (glass).

Choose a noun from the box to finish each sentence. Change the noun to mean more than one.

wolf	tooth	child

8. All the _____ had a contest.

9. They wanted to see who had lost the most _____.

10. The winner got a poster of a family of _____.

Plural Race

- Take turns with a partner.
- Roll a number cube.
  Move that many spaces.
- Spell the plural of the word on which you land. Use the word in a sentence. If you are not correct, go back 2.
- The first one to the end wins.

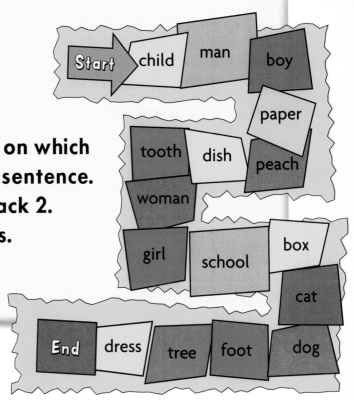

Start — child — man — boy — paper — peach — dish — tooth — woman — girl — school — box — cat — dog — foot — tree — dress — End

---

Writing Connection

Shopping List A shopping list can help you remember what to buy. Make a list of things you might buy at a store. Be sure to include the number of each thing you must buy.

Shopping List
5 pencils
2 notebooks
3 folders
4 paintbrushes

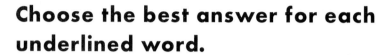

Chapter Review STANDARDIZED TEST PREP

Choose the best answer for each underlined word.

1. My brother and I like to pick fuzzy <u>peach</u>.

   a. peachs

   b. peaches

   c. correct as is

2. They grow on <u>trees</u> near our house.

   a. tree

   b. treees

   c. correct as is

3. We keep the peaches in <u>baskets</u>.

   a. basket

   b. basketes

   c. correct as is

4. My brother and I put two peaches in our lunch <u>boxs</u>.

   a. box

   b. boxes

   c. correct as is

5. I shared my fruit with <u>friendes</u> at school.

   a. friends

   b. friend

   c. correct as is

6. We bit into the fruit with our <u>toothes</u>.

   a. teeth

   b. tooths

   c. correct as is

Visit our website for more activities with plural nouns:

www.harcourtschool.com

Study Skills

Finding Words in a Dictionary

A **dictionary** is a book that gives the meanings of words. The words are in alphabetical order. To find a word, first look at the two **guide words** at the top of each page. The first guide word tells the first word on the page. The second guide word tells the last word on the page.

rabbit   **rate**

rab•bit [rab′ ət] A small animal with long ears, a short tail, and soft fur. **The *rabbit* lives in a hole.**

race [rās] A contest to find out who is fastest. **They had a *race* to the finish line.**

rack•et [rak′ ət] A loud or confusing noise. **The rain made a *racket*.**

raft [raft] A flat boat made of logs or boards tied together. **They floated down the river on a *raft*.**

Practice

Write the words that would be found on the dictionary page. Use the guide words to help you.

1. rack   2. swim   3. ramp   4. rain   5. rose

Adding Details

In a **thank-you note**, a writer thanks someone for a gift or for doing something nice. A thank-you note has five parts. The **heading** tells the writer's address and the date. The **greeting** says "hello." The **body** tells why the writer is thanking the person. The **closing** says "good-bye." Finally the **signature** tells who wrote the note.

A good writer adds **details**, or exact information, about a gift to the body of a thank-you note. Details show the reader that the writer really liked the gift.

Read the thank-you note on the next page. Look at how the writer adds details to show her thanks.

from

Kate Heads West

by Pat Brisson ◆ *illustrated by Rick Brown*

25 Abbot St.
Phillipsburg, New Jersey 08865
September 4, 2001

Dear Mr. and Mrs. Tooper,

Thanks for taking me on vacation with you. I had a great time. The things I liked best were walking to Mexico and the raft ride down the Colorado River. I also liked the cowgirls at the rodeo.

I learned a lot about Oklahoma cowboys, Texas deserts, New Mexico bats, and Arizona Indians. The best thing I learned was how lucky Lucy is to have you for parents and how lucky I am to be

Lucy's best friend,

Kate

P.S. I want you to know I wrote this thank-you note even before my mother told me to do so.

Think About It

1. Find the five parts in Kate's thank-you note.

2. What details has Kate added to show that she is truly thankful?

Writer's Craft

Adding Details

Details help readers picture what you are telling. Read these sentences.

> I learned a lot about Oklahoma, Texas, New Mexico, and Arizona.
>
> I learned a lot about Oklahoma **cowboys**, Texas **deserts**, New Mexico **bats,** and Arizona **Indians**.

The writer added details to the second sentence to help tell exactly what she means. *Cowboys*, *deserts*, *bats,* and *Indians* help make good word pictures.

Writers also add details that tell about their feelings, such as where Kate says how lucky she is to have Lucy as a best friend. These details show a writer's "voice," or personality.

A. Write each sentence. Add details to take the place of the underlined word. Use the Idea Bank for help.

1. Thank you for inviting me to the place.
2. It was great that we had seats.
3. We saw many things.
4. I loved petting the horse.
5. I still look at the picture.

Idea Bank
• prize-winning bronco
• Texas rodeo
• bronco riders
• front-row seats
• photo of me dressed for the rodeo

B. Add details to complete this thank-you note.

181 Sunny Road
Apopka, Florida 32712
November 15, 2001

Dear Jodi,

Thank you for inviting me to the fair. I had a great time. It was fun when we 1._____. I really liked the food, especially the 2._____.

I still have the 3._____ I got. It reminds me of 4._____. I hope we can do it again 5._____.

Your friend,
Kathleen

Writing and Thinking

Reflect Tell what helped you think of good details to add to the thank–you note. Write your ideas. Talk about your ideas in a small group.

Writer's Craft

Applying the Craft TAAS SKILL

Read this student thank-you note. Think about how the underlined words add details.

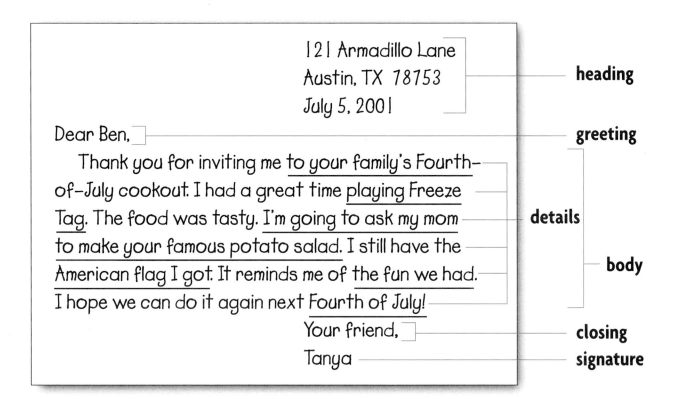

121 Armadillo Lane
Austin, TX 78753
July 5, 2001 — heading

Dear Ben, — greeting

Thank you for inviting me <u>to your family's Fourth-of-July cookout</u>. I had a great time <u>playing Freeze Tag</u>. The food was tasty. I'm going <u>to ask my mom to make your famous potato salad</u>. I still have the <u>American flag I got</u>. <u>It reminds me of the fun we had.</u> I hope we can do it again next <u>Fourth of July!</u>

— details — body

Your friend, — closing
Tanya — signature

Looking at the Model

1. Which parts of this note help make good word pictures? Why?

2. Does Tanya sound thankful? Why? How do you think Ben will feel when he reads this note? Why?

Your Turn

Write a thank-you note. Add details that show why you are thankful and how you feel.

Prewriting and Drafting

STEP 1 **Develop your ideas.**

Ask yourself these questions.

- Whom should I thank? Why am I thankful?
- What details can I add?

STEP 2 **Brainstorm details.**

Make a chart. Tell why you are thankful.

> **Whom I Want to Thank**

> **Why I Am Thankful**

> **Details About Why I Am Thankful**

STEP 3 **Write your draft.**

Use your chart and What Good Writers Do to write a draft of your thank-you note. Use words to let your personality show.

What Good Writers Do

 Plan your ideas.

 Remember to add details that show your reader why you are thankful.

✓ Add details that let your voice and personality show.

Student Handbook

Use the friendly letter checklist on page 483 to make sure you have all the parts of a good letter.

Editing Your Thank-You Note

Share your draft with a few classmates. Talk about ways to make your thank-you note better. Use the checklist and the **Editor's Marks** to help you revise your writing.

 My thank-you note tells why I am thankful. I give details that explain why I am thankful.

 My thank-you note has a heading, a greeting, a body, a closing, and a signature.

Editor's Marks	
∧	Add.
⅄	Change.
℘	Take out.
≡	Use a capital letter.
⊙	Add a period.
⬭	Check the spelling.

Sharing with Others

Meet with a partner or a small group. Share your thank-you note. Read it aloud. Then you may want to mail your thank-you note.

●Handwriting●

Using Correct Letter Spacing

It is important to write neatly so that others can read your writing. Follow this tip to make sure your letters are spaced correctly.

✔ Make sure letters are not too close together or too far apart.

correct

thank

too close

thank

too far apart

t h a n k

Write these sentences. Use your best handwriting. Remember to space your letters correctly.

Thanks! I like the shirt.

It matches my jeans.

I will wear it all the time.

What Is a Proper Noun?

Read the rhyme.

A, my name is Alice.
My friend's name is Ana.
We come from Alabama,
and we like apples.

B, my name is Bob.
My sister's name is Barbara.
We come from Boston,
and we like bread.

C, my name is Conchita.
My friend's name is Carl.
We come from California,
and we like cars.

Choose something you like. Then name places or people whose names begin with the same letter.

Some nouns begin with capital letters. These nouns are called **proper nouns**.

Special names of people, places, and animals are proper nouns.

Barbara likes books.
She comes from **Boston**.
She has a dog named **Buddy**.

Finish the rhyme by writing proper nouns.

D, my name is _____ .
My friend's name is _____ .
We come from _____ ,
and we like dinosaurs.

E, my name is _____ .
My friend's name is _____ .
We come from _____ ,
and we like eggs.

People, Places, and Animals

The special names of people, places, and animals are proper nouns. Proper nouns begin with capital letters.

Linda Miller is my favorite teacher.
My school is called **West Side School.**
Our class pet is a hamster
    named **Fuzz.**

Guided Practice

Write the proper noun in ( ) correctly. Then tell if it is a person, a place, or an animal.

1. Today my sister and I went to help (emma jones).

2. First we gave a bath to her dog (rocky).

3. Next we walked it down (fernwood street).

4. Then her daughter (kim) drove us to town.

5. She took us to (ray's pizza) for lunch.

The special names of people, places, and animals are proper nouns.

Independent Practice

Write the proper noun in ( ) correctly. Then tell if it is a person, a place, or an animal.

6. Last month my class cleaned (maple park).

7. My friend (carl) picked up some paper.

8. He found a postcard from (los angeles).

9. He also saw a ticket for a game at (ashley field).

10. (ana alonso) raked the leaves.

11. We washed benches by (sun lake).

12. (latisha) and I planted some flowers.

13. A man walked by with his dog, (rex).

14. The man's name was (alex king).

15. He went to (south school) fifty years ago!

Writing Connection

Writing Information Write important information about yourself. Write your name, the street and city where you live, the name of your school, and the name of your pet, if you have one.

To make a capital letter on the computer, hold the **shift** key and type the letter you need.

Days, Months, and Holidays

The names of days, months, and holidays are proper nouns. The names of days and months begin with capital letters.

The first **Monday** in **September** is next week.

All important words in the names of holidays begin with capital letters.

Thanksgiving and **Labor Day** are my dad's favorite holidays.

Guided Practice

Find proper nouns that should be capitalized. Write each one correctly.

1. This year I helped my family from january to december.

2. I helped Mom plan the new year's day party.

3. Then in february, I helped Dad shovel snow.

4. I did some spring cleaning in march.

5. I cleaned my room every saturday.

Independent Practice

Find proper nouns that should be capitalized. Write each one correctly.

6. In april I dug the garden with Grandpa.

7. I grew flowers for mother's day.

8. Finally school was out in june.

9. I got to wash the car every tuesday.

10. I made salad for the fourth of july picnic.

11. In august I went to the beach.

12. By labor day I was ready for school.

13. I helped Dad rake leaves in october.

14. I set the table on thanksgiving.

15. In december I decorated the house.

Writing Connection

Elaboration Draw a picture of yourself helping your family at a special time during the year. Write a caption for the picture. Use proper nouns to tell what you do, when you do it, and how doing it helps.

Use your computer's spell-check to help you make sure you capitalized all the proper nouns.

Extra Practice

Write each proper noun correctly.

1. The jackson family has many pets.

2. stan takes care of them.

3. He feeds millie the goldfish every day.

4. In the morning, he walks his dog foxy.

5. He buys dog toys in a store called doggy's.

6. That store is in mapletown.

Write the names of days, months, and holidays correctly.

7. Stan gave a treat to his dog last november.

8. One thursday he gave it some turkey.

9. The next friday he gave it some more.

10. Now his dog loves thanksgiving!

Language Play

Tic-Tac-Toe

- Each player needs 6 markers. Take turns choosing a square.
- Tell if the words are written correctly. If they are not, tell how to fix them.
- Put a marker on the square if you are right.
- The first player to get three in a row across, down, or on a slant wins.

Texas	October	sunday
Rover	Emma Hong	chicago
peter wolf	Labor Day	may

Writing Connection

Help Certificate Make a promise to do an extra chore. Put your promise in writing. Give it to a family member as a gift. Include your name and the month when you will do the chore.

I, Lisa Lynch, promise to clear the table every night for one week. I will do this chore in *November*. I'll even clean up after Thanksgiving dinner next Thursday.

Chapter Review

Choose the best answer for each underlined word or words.

1. The Jones family moved last <u>August</u>.

   a. august

   b. AugusT

   c. correct as is

2. They moved to <u>Houston, texas</u>.

   a. houston, texas

   b. Houston, Texas

   c. correct as is

3. Even little <u>ashley Jones</u> helped unpack.

   a. ashley jones

   b. Ashley Jones

   c. correct as is

4. They started unpacking on a <u>thursDay</u>.

   a. Thursday

   b. thursday

   c. correct as is

5. Their pet dog <u>Roxy</u> slept in an empty box.

   a. roxy

   b. ROxy

   c. correct as is

6. By <u>labor Day</u>, the family was moved in.

   a. Labor Day

   b. labor day

   c. correct as is

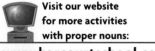

Visit our website
for more activities
with proper nouns:

www.harcourtschool.com

▣ Vocabulary ▣

Abbreviations and Titles

An **abbreviation** is a short way to write a word. It begins with a capital letter and ends with a period.

Titles		Days		Months	
Mister	**Mr.**	Sunday	**Sun.**	January	**Jan.**
Mr. Gomez		Monday	**Mon.**	February	**Feb.**
		Tuesday	**Tues.**	March	**Mar.**
Missus	**Mrs.**	Wednesday	**Wed.**	April	**Apr.**
Mrs. Reed		Thursday	**Thurs.**	May	—
		Friday	**Fri.**	June	—
Doctor	**Dr.**	Saturday	**Sat.**	July	—
Dr. Choi				August	**Aug.**
				September	**Sept.**
				October	**Oct.**
				November	**Nov.**
				December	**Dec.**

Practice

Write the abbreviation for each noun.

1. Doctor
2. Missus
3. Saturday
4. Friday
5. December
6. February

Mr. Gomez
Manager

What Is a Pronoun?

Read the poem.

Something BIG Has Been Here

Something big has been here,
what it was, I do not know,
for I did not see it coming,
and I did not see it go,
but I hope I never meet it,
if I do, I'm in a fix,
for it left behind its footprints,
they are size nine-fifty-six.

Jack Prelutsky

Talk about what the big thing in the poem could be. Then describe something to your classmates, but do not name it. Can they guess what it is?

A **pronoun** is a word that takes the place of a noun. The words **he**, **she**, **it**, and **they** are pronouns.

A **tyrannosaurus** was very big.
It was more than 45 feet long.

Write a riddle like the one below. Use pronouns. Then read it to a partner. Can your partner guess the answer?

It is large and gray.

It has a long trunk and big white tusks.

You may see it in a zoo or a circus.

What is it?

Answer: It is an elephant.

135

He, She, It, and *They*

He, *she*, *it*, and **they** are pronouns. *He* and *she* tell about other people. *It* tells about an animal or thing. *They* tells about more than one.

noun	**Matt** likes to sing.
pronoun	**He** likes to sing.
nouns	**Ken** and **Amy** practice at school.
pronoun	**They** practice at school.

Guided Practice

Write a pronoun for the word or words in ( ).

1. (The game) will be on Monday.

2. (Maria) will play catcher.

3. Can (Philip) bat first?

4. (Julia and Daniel) will play on the same team.

5. Does (Carla) want to pitch?

Independent Practice

Write a pronoun for the word or words in ( ).

6. (Christina) played first base.

7. (Tom) ran quickly.

8. (Rosa, Marta, and Tina) scored home runs.

9. At the end, (the children) ran around the bases.

10. (The parents) cheered loudly.

11. Everyone enjoyed (the game).

12. (Ms. Ortiz) was very proud of us.

13. (Jonah and Carol) want to play soccer next week.

14. (Lee) said that is a great idea.

15. (The soccer game) will be very exciting.

Writing Connection

Revising Look at a piece of your writing. Find places where you have used the same noun in two sentences in a row. Change the noun in the second sentence to a pronoun. This will make your writing smoother.

Highlight a word you want to change. Type the new word. The old word will be deleted when you type the new one.

I and *Me*

> You can use the pronouns **I** and **me** to take the place of your name when you tell about yourself. Use **I** in the naming part of a sentence. Use **me** in the telling part of a sentence.
>
> naming part   **I** play ball with Sue.
> telling part   Sue throws the ball to **me**.

Guided Practice

Write the correct word to complete each sentence.

1. (I, Me) play baseball with Dad.

2. Dad pitches the ball to (I, me).

3. (I, Me) hit the ball.

4. Dad shows (I, me) how to throw.

5. Dad and (I, me) like baseball.

Independent Practice

Write the correct word to complete each sentence.

6. My aunt and (I, me) went to a baseball game.

7. My aunt gave (I, me) the tickets to hold.

8. (I, me) gave the tickets to the man.

9. My aunt and (I, me) went inside.

10. (I, me) sat next to my aunt.

11. (I, me) cheered for our team.

12. A player gave a ball to (I, me).

13. The player told my aunt and (I, me) his name, too.

14. (I, me) showed the ball to my aunt.

15. (I, me) was very happy.

Writing Connection

Story About Me Think of something fun that you did. Write sentences that tell about it. Use _I_ or _me_ in each sentence. You may draw a picture if you want.

Extra Practice

Write the pronoun in each sentence.

1. I like books about animals.

2. They like stories about children.

3. Which story does she like best?

4. He likes books about sports.

Write a pronoun for the word or words in ( ).

5. (My sister) wants to write her own book.

6. (My parents) are both writers.

7. Did (your father) write a book for children?

8. Is (the book) at the library?

9. (My cousin Stella) found the book on the shelf.

10. (The girls) read it at home.

Write *I* or *me* to complete each sentence.

11. My mother gave (I, me) a new book.

12. (I, me) read it to my brother.

13. My brother and (I, me) like the book very much.

14. (I, me) show it to my friend.

15. My friend tells (I, me) he likes it, too.

Language Play

Pronoun Play

- Play this game with a partner.
- Make game cards like the ones here.
- Put the cards in a pile. Take turns picking a card.
- Say a pronoun for the word or words on the card. Then use the pronoun in a sentence.
- Score one point for each correct sentence you say. The first one to get five points wins.

girl

coach

game

shoes

Ramon and Joe

players

ball

Anita and Molly

goal

boys

Writing Connection

Postcard Make a postcard to send to a friend. On the front, draw a picture of something you did. On the back, write a note telling about what you did. Be sure to use pronouns correctly.

Dear Tony,
I had a great soccer game yesterday. It was a lot of fun. Tommy and I made two goals each. This picture shows me kicking a goal!
Your friend,
Pete

Tony De Luna
200 Elm Street
Brooklyn, NY 11201

Chapter Review

 **STANDARDIZED TEST PREP**

Choose the best answer for each underlined word or words.

1. The <u>pilot</u> flies the plane.

   a. They   **b.** It   **c.** She

2. The <u>plane</u> goes up high.

   a. It   **b.** He   **c.** She

3. Are <u>Carol and Bob</u> flying to Texas?

   a. they   **b.** she   **c.** he

4. On Monday <u>Bob</u> is going to Dallas.

   a. she   **b.** it   **c.** he

5. Then <u>Carol and Bob</u> are going to San Antonio.

   a. he   **b.** they   **c.** it

6. <u>My mom and I</u> flew on an airplane.

   a. Me and my mom   **b.** My mom and me   **c.** correct as is

7. She likes to travel with <u>I and my brother</u>.

   a. my brother and I   **b.** my brother and me   **c.** correct as is

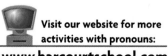 **Visit our website for more activities with pronouns:**
www.harcourtschool.com

▣ Technology ▣

Sending E-mail

You can use your computer to get and send e-mail messages. If your computer has a modem, you can send e-mail to other people who have modems.

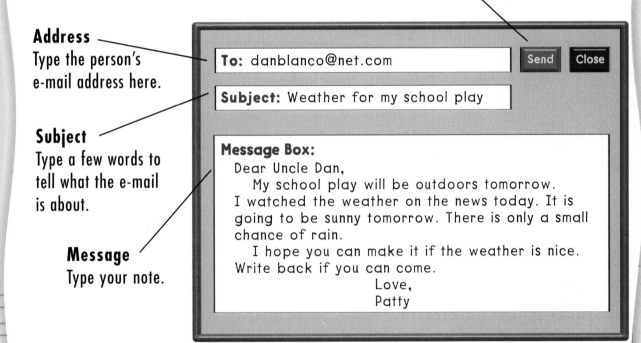

Send
Click on this to send your e-mail.

Address
Type the person's e-mail address here.

Subject
Type a few words to tell what the e-mail is about.

Message
Type your note.

To: danblanco@net.com   Send   Close

Subject: Weather for my school play

Message Box:
Dear Uncle Dan,
   My school play will be outdoors tomorrow.
I watched the weather on the news today. It is going to be sunny tomorrow. There is only a small chance of rain.
   I hope you can make it if the weather is nice. Write back if you can come.
                    Love,
                    Patty

Practice

Before you start an e-mail, ask your teacher or parent if it is all right. Remember to think about whom you would like to e-mail and what you want to say. Send an e-mail message to someone you know.

Have you ever written a friendly letter? In a friendly letter a writer writes to someone he or she knows. Think about what Rosie tells in her letter to her mother.

Don't Forget to Write

by Martina Selway

"I don't want to stay with Grandad and Aunty Mabel," Rosie said. "I don't like smelly farms. I won't have anyone to play with. I want to stay at home!"

"Come on, Rosie," Mom answered. "Grandad and Aunty Mabel haven't seen you in ages. You'll love all the animals, and you'll have lots of fun.

"Now don't forget to take baths, don't forget to wash your hair, don't forget to brush your teeth, and . . . don't forget to write."

Griggs Farm
Manchester, Vermont 05254
June 1, 2001

Dear Mom,

I didn't want you to leave me at Grandad's. When you left, I cried and cried.

Grandad said, "Come on Old Ginger Nut, dry those tears and let's see if Aunty Mabel has made us a snack."

I don't like being called "Old Ginger Nut." I want to come home.

145

Aunty Mabel made some toast on the fire, and I had one of her special raisin cookies. It was very hard.

Grandad said, "Don't drop it on the floor. It'll crack the tiles."

My wobbly tooth came out. I want to come home.

After dinner I explored in Grandad's big cabinets. There was so much to look at that I stayed up really late.

I told Grandad that I was searching for buried treasure.

Grandad said, "You're just like your Mom, Old Ginger Nut, silly as a goose."

I found some funny old pictures of you. I can bring them with me when I come home.

Grandad took me fishing in the river this afternoon. I waited for ages and ages, but he didn't catch a fish. I got fed up and made a dam with the stones.

Grandad said, "Just hold your horses. We'll have a fish as big as a whale in a minute."

Aunty Mabel cooked fish sticks for dinner. I wish we had a river at home.

Aunty Mabel made us a picnic today because we had a long climb up the hill to fetch the sheep. It was very hot. All we could hear were sheep munching grass and bees buzzing.

Grandad said, "It's going to be a lot quieter next week without you buzzing around!"

I can't believe there are only two days left before I have to come home.

Grandad said, "It's time we mailed that letter. I thought you were writing a book. It's taken you so long!"

PLEASE let me stay a little longer with Grandad. I don't want to come home yet.

Lots of love,
Old Ginger Nut _X

Griggs Farm
Manchester, Vermont 05254

Ms. A. Lee
1764 Hill Road
Hartford, Connecticut 06160

Think About It

1. What is the most interesting thing Rosie writes in her letter to her mom? Tell why.

2. How do Rosie's feelings change from the beginning of the letter to the end? How do you know?

Parts of a Letter

A friendly letter has five parts.

1. The **heading** tells the date and sometimes the writer's address.

2. The **greeting** says hello.

3. The **body** is the friendly message.

4. The **closing** says good-bye.

5. The **signature** is the writer's handwritten name.

On a sheet of paper, write the five parts of Rosie's letter. For the body of the letter, write a sentence that tells why she wrote.

Heading

Greeting
Dear_____ ,

Body

Closing
Signature

A Student Model TAAS SKILL

Ramon wrote a letter to his Uncle Pablo. He made sure his letter had all of the correct parts. Read the letter, and look for the important parts.

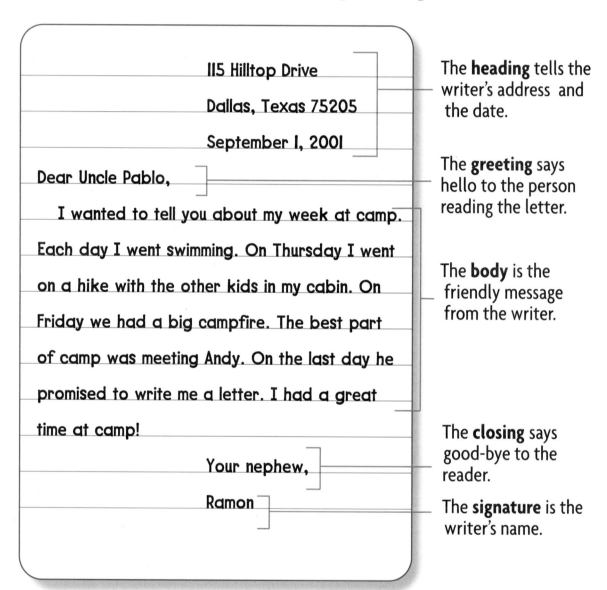

115 Hilltop Drive

Dallas, Texas 75205

September 1, 2001

The **heading** tells the writer's address and the date.

Dear Uncle Pablo,

The **greeting** says hello to the person reading the letter.

I wanted to tell you about my week at camp. Each day I went swimming. On Thursday I went on a hike with the other kids in my cabin. On Friday we had a big campfire. The best part of camp was meeting Andy. On the last day he promised to write me a letter. I had a great time at camp!

The **body** is the friendly message from the writer.

Your nephew,

The **closing** says good-bye to the reader.

Ramon

The **signature** is the writer's name.

Looking at the Model

1. What is Ramon's address?
   When does he write the letter?

2. To whom is Ramon writing?

3. What does Ramon do at camp on Thursday?
   What does he do on Friday?

4. What else happens at camp?

5. How does Ramon feel about camp?
   How do you know?

Writer's Craft

Thinking About Your Audience

Ramon wrote his letter to his favorite uncle. He used friendly words and told about interesting things. Find the parts of Ramon's letter that Uncle Pablo would enjoy reading.

- What does Ramon want to tell Uncle Pablo?

- Why does he say what he did on different days?

- What was the best part of Ramon's week?

- How does Ramon let Uncle Pablo know he had fun?

Prewriting

Ramon enjoyed reading Rosie's letter. That was when he decided to write to his Uncle Pablo, who lived far away. He drew pictures of what he wanted to share with his uncle. Ramon decided to tell about camp because he had such a good time there.

Ramon planned the body of his letter. He used a web to help him decide what to write.

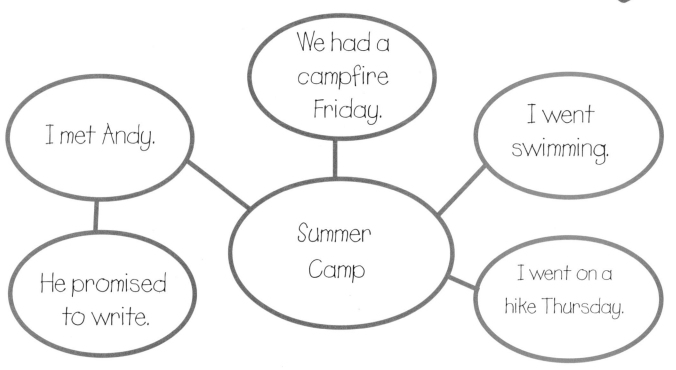

We had a campfire Friday.

I met Andy.

I went swimming.

Summer Camp

He promised to write.

I went on a hike Thursday.

Your Turn

STEP 1 **Choose a person to whom you would like to write.**

STEP 2 **Decide why you are writing.**
Think about what you want to tell this person. Draw pictures if you want.

STEP 3 **Make a web.**
Plan what you will write in your letter.

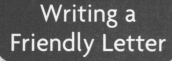

Drafting

To start his letter, Ramon wrote the heading
and greeting. Then he used his web to help him
begin writing the body. Last he will add the
closing and signature. He writes everything
quickly to get down the most important ideas.
He knows he can fix any mistakes later.

DRAFT

115 Hilltop Drive

Dallas, Texas 75205

September 1, 2001

Dear Uncle Pablo,

    I wanted to tell you about my week at camp.

Each day I went swimming. On Thursday I went

on a hike with the other kids in my cabin. The

best part of camp was meeting Andy. On

the last day he promised to write

Read the first draft of Ramon's letter. Look at his web. What else can he tell Uncle Pablo about camp?

I met Andy.

We had a campfire Friday.

I went swimming.

He promised to write.

Summer Camp

I went on a hike Thursday.

Your Turn

Use your web and What Good Writers Do to write a draft of your letter.

When you write on your computer, remember to save your work often.

Revising

Ramon read his draft to a group. They talked about how to make the letter better. Ramon added more details he thought his uncle would like to know. See how Ramon **revised** his letter.

✓ Make sure your letter has all five parts. Are there any parts you need to add?

✓ Check whether your letter follows your plan. Add details if you need to do so.

(DRAFT)

115 Hilltop Drive

Dallas, Texas 75205

September 1, 2001

Dear Uncle Pablo,

I wanted to tell you about my week at camp.

Each day I went swimming. On Thursday I went

On Friday we had a big campfire.

on a hike with the other kids in my cabin. The

best part of camp was meeting Andy. On

the last day he promised to write I a letter.

i had a geat time at camp!

your nephew

Ramon

Editor's Marks

∧ Add.

⋏ Change.

℘ Take out.

Your Turn

Read your letter in a group. Use What Good Writers Do and the Editor's Marks to make it better.

Proofreading

Ramon read his letter again to look for mistakes. Why did Ramon make the changes in red?

DRAFT

115 Hilltop Drive

Dallas, Texas 75205

September 1, 2001

Dear Uncle Pablo,

I wanted to tell you about my week at camp.

Each day I went swimming. On Thursday I went

On Friday we had a big campfire.

on a hike with the other kids in my cabin. ∧ The

best part of camp was meeting Andy. On

_me_

the last day he promised to write ⟨I⟩ a letter.

great

i had a (geat) time at camp!

your nephew ∧,

Ramon

Your Turn

Now read your letter one more time. Use What Good Writers Do and the Editor's Marks to fix any mistakes.

Print your draft. Mark any mistakes on paper. Then type the corrections and print again.

Publishing

Ramon wrote a final draft of his letter. He drew pictures of camp and mailed them with the letter.

Y☺ur Turn

Write your letter neatly on a clean sheet of paper. Remember to make all the changes. Use a computer if you want. Here are some ways to make your letter fun to read.

- **Make stationery.**
  Decorate the edges of paper with drawings, stickers, or rubber stamps. Then write your letter on the stationery.

- **Send e-mail.**
  If your school has e-mail, you can send the letter using a computer. Type your letter in a document. Find out the e-mail address of the person to whom you are writing. Get permission from your teacher to send the e-mail. Then e-mail the letter to that person.

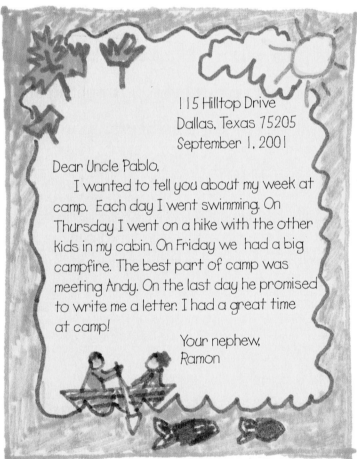

Add your finished letter to your Writing Portfolio.

Listening and Speaking

Making Introductions

When you bring together two people who do not know each other, you tell them each other's names, or **introduce** them.

Tips for Making Introductions

- When you introduce an adult to a child, speak to the adult first.

- When you introduce two friends, the order in which you introduce them does not matter.

Tips for Being Introduced

- Listen for the other person's name. Use the person's name when you first speak.

- When you are introduced, you can say, "It's nice to meet you."

Nouns for People, Places, Animals, and Things pages 98–99

Write each sentence. Underline each noun that names a person, place, or thing.

1. My family is moving from the city.

2. Our new house is by a large lake.

3. The movers are unloading the van.

4. My brother is unpacking his games.

Using Possessive Nouns pages 100–101

Use 's to rewrite the underlined words.

5. The teddy bear of Ann is missing.

6. It isn't in the crib of my sister.

7. It isn't in the toy box of Jimmy.

8. Maybe it's still in the car of my mom.

Making Nouns Plural pages 108–109

Write the correct noun that names more than one.

9. I unpacked two (boxs, boxes) of books.

10. Mom put away the (dishs, dishes).

11. Dad is looking for his (tools, tooles).

Plural Nouns That Change Spelling
pages 110–111

Write the noun in ( ) to mean more than one.

12. I brush all my (tooth) twice each day.

13. All the (child) here do this.

People, Places, and Animals pages 126–127
Write the proper noun in ( ) correctly. Then write if it is a person, a place, or an animal.

14. Our neighbor (mike ross) has a boat.

15. He took us sailing on (pine lake).

16. Our dog (spike) jumped in.

Days, Months, and Holidays pages 128–129
Write each proper noun correctly.

17. Our family moved to the lake in july.

18. Today is the last friday in august.

19. Next monday is labor day.

20. We start school on september 10.

He, She, It, and *They* pages 136–137
Write a pronoun for the words in ( ).

21. (Our new school) is five miles away.

22. (My brother Jimmy) is in third grade.

23. (My sister) isn't in school yet.

24. (Mom and Dad) are teachers.

I and *Me* pages 138–139
Write the correct pronoun in ( ) to complete each sentence.

25. (I, me) gave Spike a bath yesterday.

26. My brother Jimmy helped (I, me).

27. Jimmy and (I, me) had to catch Spike.

28. Spike ran away from Jimmy and (I, me).

Social Studies

What Do Students Read?

What do children in your school want to read? Work with classmates to find out. Then help your librarian plan what books to get.

Plan Your Research

- Decide whom to ask. Do you want to find out about one grade or about the whole school?

- Brainstorm questions about books children like to read.

- What does your librarian want to find out from children? List his or her ideas.

- Make up a form. Be sure your questions are easy to answer. Leave space on the form for children to write other ideas about books, too.

Put a check (✓) in the box (☐) to show your answer for each question.

How much do you like to read about each topic?

	a lot	some	not at all
animals	☐	☐	☐
faraway places	☐	☐	☐

Do you think the school library needs more books on each topic?

	yes, a lot more	yes, a few more	no, it has enough
animals	☐	☐	☐
faraway places	☐	☐	☐

Do you have other ideas about books? Write them on the line.

Get Information and Put It Together

- Ask each child to fill out a question form.

- Take notes to keep track of the answers.

- Plan a good way to show the librarian all of the answers to the questions.

- Count the answers to each question. Use these numbers to make a bar graph on a computer.

- List the other ideas children have about books. Then write sentences that tell the main ideas of what you learned.

Present Your Information to the Librarian

- Speak slowly and clearly. Use the bar graphs and what you wrote to help you present the information.

- Answer any questions.

Books to Read

How a Book Is Made
by Aliki
Nonfiction
This book tells how to make a book, beginning with writing and creating the pictures.
Notable Book in the Language Arts, Children's Choice

Check It Out!
by Gail Gibbons
Nonfiction
Find out how libraries help people find the books and other information they need.
Award-Winning Author

Cumulative Review
Units 1–2

Unit I: Sentences

Sentences pages 24–29

Write each group of words in an order that makes sense. Begin and end each sentence correctly.

1. tomorrow birthday is Amy's

2. to buy her a present Ken wants

3. walks he to the store

4. store has the books for children

Naming Parts and Telling Parts pages 36–37

Write each sentence. Circle the naming part. Underline the telling part.

5. Amy and Ken like books about animals.

6. Ken chooses a book about dogs.

7. The book has many nice pictures.

8. The clerk puts the book in a bag.

Kinds of Sentences pages 52–55, 64–65

Change each sentence into the kind of sentence shown in ( ). Write the new sentence.

9. You like books about animals. *(question)*

10. Can you read this book? *(command)*

11. This picture is really great. *(exclamation)*

12. It looks like your dog. *(question)*

Unit 2: Nouns

Nouns   pages 96–97, 124–125

Write each sentence. Underline each noun. Then write if it is a person, a place, an animal, or a thing.

13. Our family is going to the country.

14. My mom helps us pack our clothes.

15. Dad puts our suitcase in the car.

16. Our dog and cat are going, too.

Using Possessive Nouns   pages 100–101

Use 's to rewrite the underlined words.

17. The toys of the dog are in a bag.

18. The bed of the cat is in the trunk.

19. Mom has the map of Dad.

He, *She*, *It*, and *They*   pages 136–137

Write a pronoun for the underlined word or words.

20. Mom and Dad take turns driving.

21. My brother Tony points to a lake.

22. The lake is where we are headed.

23. My sister can hardly wait to get there.

I and *Me*   pages 138–139

Write the correct pronoun in ( ) to complete each sentence.

24. (I, me) ran to the edge of the lake.

25. My brother splashed (I, me) with water.

Unit 3

Grammar
- Verbs

Writing
- Dialogue
- Story

What Is a Verb?

Read the poem.

~On Our Way~

What kind of walk shall we take today?
Leap like a frog? Creep like a snail?
Scamper like a squirrel with a funny tail?

Flutter like a butterfly? Chicken peck?
Stretch like a turtle with a poking out neck?

Trot like a pony, clip clop clop?
Swing like a monkey in a treetop?

Scuttle like a crab? Kangaroo jump?
Plod like a camel with an up and down hump?

We could even try a brand-new way—
walking down the street
on our own two feet.

Eve Merriam

Show or tell about ways you can walk. Then write words that tell about other ways you can move.

> A **verb** can tell about an action that happens now.
>
> I **leap** like a frog.
> I **creep** like a snail.

Write a verb and an animal name in each item to add new lines for the poem.

Gallop like a horse ?

_____ like a _____?
_____ like a _____?
_____ like a _____?
_____ like a _____?
_____ like a _____?

Adding *s* or *es* to Verbs

Add **s** to most verbs to tell what one
person or thing does now.

  Mr. Bing **feeds** the animals
  in the pet shop.

Add **es** if the verb ends in **ss**, **ch**,
sh, or **x**.

  Mrs. Bing **brushes** the dogs.

Guided Practice

Write the correct verb to finish each sentence.

  1. The Bings (bring, brings) pets to the park.

  2. One rabbit (eat, eats) food.

  3. Then it (hop, hops) out of its cage.

  4. Nina and Jean (spot, spots) the rabbit.

  5. Nina (catch, catches) it.

Independent Practice

Write the correct verb to finish each sentence.

6. Mr. and Mrs. Bing (train, trains) animals.

7. Mrs. Bing (give, gives) a rabbit to the girls.

8. The girls (thank, thanks) Mrs. Bing.

9. Animals (help, helps) people in different ways.

10. Coco (open, opens) doors for Jim.

11. Rover (fetch, fetches) things for Claire.

12. He (kiss, kisses) Claire with a big lick.

13. The guide dog (lead, leads) a girl.

14. The girl and the dog (walk, walks) across the street.

15. Animals and people (work, works) as a team.

Writing Connection

Using Exact Words Draw a picture of animals at a pet store. Write sentences. Use verbs to tell exactly what the animals are doing.

Use your computer to write and print out your sentences.

Combining Sentences with Verbs

> The naming parts of two sentences are sometimes the same. You can join the sentences by using **and**. This can make your writing easier to read and understand.
>
> Molly looks in the bush.
> Molly sees a bird.
>
> Molly looks in the bush **and** sees a bird.

Guided Practice

Use *and* to join each pair of sentences. Write the new sentence.

1. The ranger drives the jeep.
   The ranger watches for animals.

2. We go on a tour.
   We see many squirrels.

3. The squirrels carry nuts.
   The squirrels climb trees.

4. We find deer tracks.
   We spot two deer.

Independent Practice

Use *and* to join each pair of sentences. Write the new sentence.

5. Chris brushes the horses.
   Chris cleans the stable.

6. Von washes dogs.
   Von clips their nails.

7. Vets help sick animals.
   Vets check healthy animals.

8. Tanya cares for bees.
   Tanya collects honey.

9. Rangers help wild animals.
   Rangers teach about animals.

10. Some scientists study the ocean.
    Some scientists learn about fish.

Writing Connection

Revising Look through your Writing Portfolio. Choose one piece of writing. Find the naming parts in your sentences. Which sentences could you combine? Revise your writing.

Use your computer to help you combine sentences.

Extra Practice

Write the verb in each sentence.

1. Mia calls her cats Fred and Barney.

2. Fred eats all the time.

3. Barney sleeps most of the day.

4. The two cats race all around the house.

**Write the verb in ( ) to finish each sentence.
Add *s* or *es* if you need to.**

5. Mia and little Paco (play) with the cats.

6. Mia (tell) Paco to be careful.

7. Paco (touch) the cats gently.

8. Fred and Barney (purr) happily.

**Read each pair of sentences. Use *and*
to join them. Write the new sentence.**

9. The cat meows.
   The cat jumps on Mia's lap.

10. Barney jumps up.
    Barney knocks over a cup.

Language Play

Roll a Verb

- Take turns with a partner. Roll two number cubes. Add up the numbers.
- Use the verb in a sentence. You get one point for each verb used correctly.
- The first player with five points wins.

brush 2	
hug 3	**watch** 4
feed 5	**teach** 6
comb 7	**wash** 8
hold 9	**train** 10
bark 11	**climb** 12

Writing Connection

Functional Writing: To-Do List A to-do list can help you remember what you have to do. Make your own to-do list. Begin each sentence in the list with an action verb.

To Do

- See Mrs. Ralph about the art show.
- Play soccer at 3:30.
- Meet Mom at her office at 5:00.
- Write spelling words before dinner.

Chapter Review

Choose the correct answer for each underlined word.

1. Dr. Jackson <u>works</u> in an animal hospital.

   a. work

   b. workes

   c. correct as is

2. Maria <u>tell</u> the vet that Gus cut his leg.

   a. tells

   b. telles

   c. correct as is

3. She and the nurse <u>wash</u> Gus's cut.

   a. washs

   b. washes

   c. correct as is

4. Then Dr. Jackson <u>stitch</u> the cut.

   a. stitchs

   b. stitches

   c. correct as is

Use *and* to join the pair of sentences. Write the new sentence.

5. Maria gives Gus a treat. Maria takes him home.

6. Gus feels better now. Gus wags his tail.

**Visit our website
for more activities
with verbs:**

www.harcourtschool.com

Vocabulary

Synonyms for Verbs

A **synonym** is a word that means the same or almost the same as another word. Using synonyms for some verbs can make your writing more interesting.

They **walk** to the lake.
They **march** to the lake.
They **stroll** to the lake.

Practice

Write two synonyms for each underlined verb. Then choose one synonym, and rewrite the sentence.

1. A bear and her cubs <u>run</u> to the lake.

2. The bear <u>gets</u> some fish.

3. The cubs <u>look</u> at her.

4. The bears <u>jump</u> on a rock.

5. Then they all <u>eat</u> the fish.

Verbs That Tell About the Past

Read the poem.

Tommy

I put a seed into the ground
And said, "I'll watch it grow."
I watered it and cared for it
As well as I could know.

One day I walked in my backyard,
And oh, what did I see!
My seed had popped itself right out,
Without consulting me.

Gwendolyn Brooks

consulting

**Think about something you did.
Maybe you planted a seed or made a
craft. Show or tell about what happened.
Then write verbs that tell what happened.**

A **verb** can tell about an action that
happened in the past.

Last week I **played** in my backyard.

I **watered** the plant yesterday.

**Write a verb that tells about the past in
each sentence.**

Last spring I _____ seeds.

I _____ the dirt.

I _____ all the weeds.

Every day I _____ the seeds.

At last a plant _____ up.

Adding *ed* to Verbs

> Many verbs end with **ed** to tell about something that happened in the past.
>
> Last night I **cleaned** my tent.
>
> Yesterday I **fished** in the river.

Guided Practice

Write the verb that tells about the past.

1. Yesterday we (walked, walk) up a steep mountain.

2. In the morning I (pack, packed) my backpack.

3. I (stuffed, stuff) a sweater into the backpack.

4. I (added, add) a bottle of water.

5. We (climb, climbed) all afternoon.

Many verbs end with *ed* to tell about something that happened in the past.

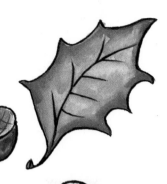

Independent Practice

Write the verb that tells about the past.

6. Ned (leaps, leaped) over logs.

7. Sara (gathered, gathers) acorns.

8. Everyone (collects, collected) leaves from the ground.

9. We (jumped, jump) on rocks near the river.

10. We (rest, rested) for an hour.

11. Ned (fished, fishes) in the river.

12. He (pulls, pulled) out a little fish.

13. Ned (tossed, toss) it back into the water.

14. Then the wind (turns, turned) cold.

15. We (walk, walked) back down the mountain.

Writing Connection

Writing a Journal Entry Think about a walk you have taken. Draw pictures that show things you did. Write a sentence about each picture. Use verbs that show that the actions happened in the past.

Save your work on your computer. You can add more details later.

Changing Verbs That End with *e*

> If a verb ends with the letter **e**, drop the **e** before adding **ed**.
>
> They **like** red leaves.
> Last fall they **liked** red leaves.
>
> I **rake** the leaves.
> Last week I **raked** the leaves.

Guided Practice

Write the verb in ( ) to tell about the past.

1. The hikers (hope) for a sunny day.

2. Mom (pile) wood on the fire.

3. Dad (place) a pan of water on the fire.

4. Karen (share) her bread with the birds.

5. They (hike) all day.

Independent Practice

Write the verb in ( ) to tell about the past.

6. The family (like) to hike early.

7. They (line) up to walk on the trail.

8. Mark (time) the hike with his watch.

9. Mom saw a nest where a bird (live).

10. Karen (love) the birds.

11. She (surprise) the bird with a piece of bread.

12. She (save) the bread from breakfast.

13. The family (arrive) at the tent on time.

14. Mark (dance) because he was glad.

15. Everyone (celebrate).

Writing Connection

Revising Look through your Writing Portfolio. Choose a story. Check the past-tense verbs to make sure you wrote them correctly.

You can highlight incorrect past-tense verbs with your mouse and then type in the correct verb.

Extra Practice

Read each sentence. Write the verb that tells about the past.

1. It snowed outside last night.

2. We picked up our backpacks.

3. Dad opened the cabin door.

Write the verb in ( ) that tells about the past.

4. Ted (watches, watched) the snowflakes.

5. Mom (mixes, mixed) the hot chocolate.

6. We (listened, listens) to stories.

Write the verb in ( ) to tell about the past.

7. Kendra (tape) the stories.

8. She (invite) Ted to help.

9. Ted (hope) to hike in the snow.

10. Kendra (promise) to go with him.

Language Play

Act Out the Past

- Think of something you did in the past week.
- Act it out for a classmate.
- Have the classmate guess what you did. Tell about it, using past-tense verbs.
- Then have your classmate act out something for you to guess.

Writing Connection

A Friendly Letter Write a letter to a friend. Tell your friend what you did this past weekend. Remember to write your verbs in the past tense. Use the following letter as a model.

62 Sea Drive

Orlando, Florida 32887

March 5, 200–

Dear Sal,

On Saturday I cleaned my room. Then I helped my dad fix my bike. I played in a basketball game, too. Later my whole family watched a great movie. What did you do over the weekend?

Your friend,

Pete

Chapter Review STANDARDIZED TEST PREP

Choose the sentence that tells about something that happened in the past.

1. Jane enjoy her camping trip.

   a. Jane enjoyed her camping trip.

   b. Jane enjoys her camping trip.

   c. correct as is

2. She liked the walks in the woods.

   a. She likes the walks in the woods.

   b. She like the walks in the woods.

   c. correct as is

3. Jane watch a deer.

   a. Jane watches a deer.

   b. Jane watched a deer.

   c. correct as is

4. She followed a rabbit.

   a. She following a rabbit.

   b. She follows a rabbit.

   c. correct as is

5. Her friends walk with her.

   a. Her friends walked with her.

   b. Her friends walking with her.

   c. correct as is

6. They prepare sandwiches for lunch.

   a. They prepares sandwiches for lunch.

   b. They prepared sandwiches for lunch.

   c. correct as is

Visit our website for more activities with past-tense verbs:
www.harcourtschool.com

▣ Study Skills ▣

Using a Dictionary Entry

The words in dark print in a dictionary are called **entry words**. The entry words are listed in alphabetical order. If a word has more than one meaning, the meanings are numbered. Sometimes an example sentence is given to make a meaning clearer.

entry word — **pick** [pik] **1.** To choose: **We *pick* a movie we like. 2.** To eat without being hungry: **Sometimes I *pick* at my supper.**

meaning

example sentence

Practice

Use the dictionary entry to answer the questions.

1. What is the first meaning of the verb *pick*?

2. What is the second meaning of *pick*?

3. Which entry word would come after *pick—pen*, *pie*, or *paddle*?

4. What is the example sentence for the first meaning of *pick*?

5. Write your own example sentence for the second meaning of *pick*.

Writer's Craft

Using Quotations to Show Feeling

Many stories have dialogue. In **dialogue**, a writer tells the exact words that characters say to each other. Dialogue helps readers better understand what the characters are like.

In dialogue, a character's exact words are placed inside **quotation marks** (" "). A word such as *said* or *cried* is in the sentence to tell how the character said the words.

Read this dialogue. How do the characters' words help you know what they are like?

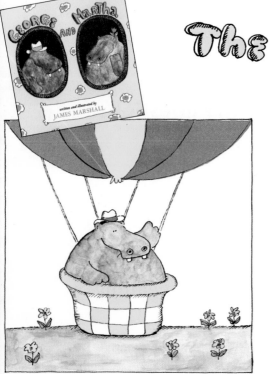

The Flying Machine

from *George and Martha*
by James Marshall

"I'm going to be the first of my species to fly!" said George.

"Then why aren't you flying?" asked Martha. "It seems to me that you are still on the ground."

"You are right," said George. "I don't seem to be going anywhere at all."

"Maybe the basket is too heavy," said Martha.

"Yes," said George, "I think you are right again. Maybe if I climb out, the basket will be lighter."

"Oh dear!" cried George. "Now what have I done? There goes my flying machine!"

"That's all right," said Martha. "I would rather have you down here with me."

With a partner, read the dialogue aloud as if you were George and Martha talking to each other. Read only the character's exact words.

Think About It

1. How do Martha and George feel about each other? How do you know?

2. How could you tell who was talking in this dialogue?

191

Writer's Craft

Using Quotations to Show Feeling

Dialogue helps readers know what characters are like and what they feel. Quotation marks show where each speaker's exact words begin and end. Writers try to make characters sound like real people talking by using everyday language. Exact verbs such as *cried* give clues about how characters feel.

"Oh dear!" cried George. "Now what have I done? There goes my flying machine!"

"That's all right," said Martha.

A. What words could you say for each of these feelings? Write a sentence to tell your exact words.

1. hurt *"Ouch! That stings."* 2. happy   3. sad

4. angry   5. surprised   6. scared

B. Write an exact verb for each sentence in Part A to tell how you would say it. Use the Word Bank or your thesaurus.

"Ouch! That stings," I yelled.

Word Bank	
asked	whispered
screamed	cried
yelled	shouted
called	whined

C. Read the paragraph below. Then write sentences for it as dialogue. A sample dialogue has been started for you.

Clyde's tail was stuck in the door. He asked Midge for help. She thought that maybe opening the door would help. Clyde thought that was a good idea. Midge opened the door so Clyde could get his tail out. Then she asked if his tail felt better. Clyde said it did and thanked Midge for her help.

"Ow!" yelled Clyde.
"What's wrong?" asked Midge.

Writing and Thinking

Reflect Tell what helped you write the paragraph as dialogue. Write your ideas. Share your ideas in a small group.

Writer's Craft

Applying the Craft

Read this dialogue a second grader wrote. Think about how the dialogue shows the characters' feelings.

here

there

The Riddle

"What a great day this is!" Chris said smiling. "The sun is out. The birds are singing."

"That makes me think of a riddle," said Mike.

"Oh, no," Chris groaned. "Not one of your riddles again!"

"Three birds sat on the fence," Mike said. "Now what is the difference between *here* and *there?*"

Looking at the Model

1. How do Chris and Mike feel at different parts of the dialogue? How do you know? Which words give clues about how the characters feel?

2. When have you felt the way the characters do? Do you think the writer has felt the same way, too? Why or why not?

Your Turn

Write a dialogue for your classmates about two characters and something funny that happened to them.

Prewriting and Drafting

STEP 1 **Develop your ideas.**

Think of two interesting characters. What are they like? What problem might they have?

STEP 2 **Brainstorm what your characters would say to each other.**

Draw pictures of your characters. Think about how they feel. Write words they would say.

STEP 3 **Write a draft of your dialogue.**

Use What Good Writers Do to help you. Include dialogue that helps the reader understand what each character is like.

What Good Writers Do

✓ Think about for whom you are writing and why.

Student Handbook

Use your Thesaurus to help you find just the right words to use in your dialogue.

Editing Your Dialogue

Read your dialogue with a partner or a group of classmates. Talk about ways to make it better. Use the checklist and the Editor's Marks to help you revise it.

Editor's Marks

⋀	Change.
ℯ	Take out.
=	Use a capital letter.
⌃,	Add a comma.
⌄"	Add quotation marks.

 My dialogue uses everyday language and tells what the characters are feeling.

 My dialogue uses quotation marks around the speakers' exact words.

 The quotations are written correctly.

Sharing with Others

Meet with a partner or small group. Share your dialogue. Read it aloud. Use your voice to show how each speaker would say the quotations.

Handwriting

Using Margins and Correct Word and Sentence Spacing

Make sure you put enough space along the side of your paper and between words and sentences. Follow these tips.

- Begin writing to the right of the red line. Leave a pencil space.

- The space between words and sentences should be as wide as a pencil.

He ran. Then he jumped.

Write these sentences. Use your best handwriting. Follow the tips to leave enough space.

Kim talked.

She told a story.

Dad liked it.

The Verbs *Am*, *Is*, and *Are*

Read the poem.

I Am Running in a Circle

I am running in a circle
and my feet are getting sore,
and my head is
spinning
spinning
as it's never spun before.
I am
dizzy
dizzy
dizzy.
Oh! I cannot bear much more.
I am trapped in a
revolving
. . . volving
. . . volving
. . . volving door!

Jack Prelutsky

198

Use the words *am*, *is*, and *are* to tell about the poem and about what might happen next.

Some verbs do not show action. They tell what someone or something is like.

I **am** very dizzy.
She **is** tired of spinning.
My feet **are** sore.

Write about how you would feel if you were going around and around in a circle.

I am upset from going around

around

around

around.

I am _____

_____

_____

_____.

I am _____

_____

_____

_____!

Using *Am*, *Is*, and *Are*

Some verbs do not show action. They tell what someone or something is like. The verbs **am**, **is**, and **are** tell about now.

I **am** seven years old.

Use	With	Example
am	I	I **am** tall.
is	nouns that name one	The bird **is** yellow.
are	nouns that name more than one	Many birds **are** brown.

Guided Practice

Choose the correct verb to finish each sentence.

1. I (am, is, are) outside with my Aunt Sue.

2. The weather (am, is, are) warm.

3. We (am, is, are) by the pond.

4. Aunt Sue (am, is, are) glad the sky is sunny.

5. I (am, is, are) happy to be with her.

Independent Practice

Choose the correct verb to finish each sentence.

6. Two frogs (am, is, are) by the pond.

7. One frog (am, is, are) green.

8. Many fish (am, is, are) in the water.

9. They (am, is, are) brown and red.

10. I (am, is, are) in a boat with Aunt Sue.

11. Aunt Sue (am, is, are) a teacher.

12. Today I (am, is, are) Aunt Sue's student.

13. She (am, is, are) here to teach me about pond animals.

14. Some ducks (am, is, are) near the boat now.

15. I (am, is, are) happy to learn about ducks.

Writing Connection

Write About Yourself Draw a picture of yourself and some classmates. Then write sentences that tell what you are like. Check to see if you used *am, is,* and *are* correctly.

You can choose different fonts, or letter styles, to write and print out your sentences.

Using *Was* and *Were*

> The verbs **was** and **were** tell what someone or something was like. They tell about the past.
>
> Use **was** with nouns that name one.
>
>   Yesterday the girl **was** happy.
>
> Use **were** with nouns that name more than one.
>
>   Last night the girls **were** tired.

Guided Practice

Write *was* or *were* to complete each sentence.

1. My parents and I _____ at the beach last Saturday.

2. My towel _____ warm.

3. The waves _____ low.

4. The water _____ cool.

5. I _____ glad to find shells.

Remember *Was* and *were* tell about the past.

Independent Practice

Write *was* or *were* to complete each sentence.

6. Yesterday the beach _____ clean.

7. The ocean _____ blue.

8. My parents _____ with me.

9. We _____ happy to be outside.

10. I _____ interested in the animals on the sand.

11. Some shells _____ white.

12. A crab _____ next to the shells.

13. The crab's two front claws _____ big.

14. Many birds _____ on the beach, too.

15. The beach _____ full of life!

Writing Connection

Using the Right Verbs Imagine you went to the beach or a lake last summer. Write sentences to tell about what you saw there. Be sure to use *was* and *were* correctly.

Change *is* to *was* by going to the **Edit** menu and clicking on **Replace**.

Extra Practice

Write *am*, *is*, or *are* to finish each sentence.

1. The birds _____ very loud.

2. They _____ on the beach.

3. This bird _____ hungry.

4. I _____ hungry, too!

Write *was* or *were* to finish each sentence.

5. My parents _____ on the beach blanket.

6. Mom _____ reading a book.

7. A crab _____ next to her foot.

Read each sentence. Write the correct verb to complete it.

is	am	are	was	were

8. I _____tired now.

9. Last week the beach _____ quiet.

10. Now we _____ back home.

Language Play

Picture Talk

- Bring in or draw two pictures of yourself. One should show you as you are now. The other should show you as a baby.
- Show one picture and tell about yourself. Then tell about the other picture.
- Be sure to use *is, am, are, was,* and *were* correctly.

Writing Connection

Write a Description Think about a person or animal you know well. Write sentences that tell about what he or she is like. Check to be sure you used the verbs *am, is, are, was,* and *were* correctly.

My Cat Tiger

My cat's name is Tiger. Tiger is black and white. His eyes are yellow, and his nose is pink. His claws are sharp. Tiger was funny when he was a kitten. He still likes to play.

Chapter Review

STANDARDIZED TEST PREP

Choose the best answer for each underlined word.

1. My red bag <u>are</u> packed.

   a. am

   b. is

   c. correct as is

2. I <u>am</u> ready to go.

   a. is

   b. are

   c. correct as is

3. My two brothers <u>is</u> ready.

   a. are

   b. am

   c. correct as is

4. Last year we <u>are</u> not ready.

   a. was

   b. were

   c. correct as is

5. My father <u>are</u> upset with us.

   a. was

   b. were

   c. correct as is

6. We missed the train because we <u>were</u> late.

   a. was

   b. is

   c. correct as is

7. We <u>is</u> not late today.

   a. was

   b. are

   c. correct as is

8. We <u>was</u> on the train!

   a. are

   b. is

   c. correct as is

Visit our website for more activities with verbs:
www.harcourtschool.com

◼ Study Skills ◼

Taking a Test

Many schools give language tests. Here are the parts of one kind of test.

directions — **Choose the best answer for each underlined word.**

item — **1.** Many shells <u>was</u> pink. ← important word

    a. is **b.** were **c.** correct as is — answer choices

Follow these tips when you take a test.

- Read or listen to all the directions.
- Plan your time. Answer the easy items first. Then go back and do the hard ones.
- Find the important word or words in the item. This will help you choose the right answer.
- Read all the answer choices. Then you can choose the best one.

Practice

Read each sentence. Write _True_ if it is true. Write _False_ if it is not true.

1. Before you start a test, read all the directions.

2. The directions tell how to do the test.

3. You should answer the hard questions first.

4. You should read all the answers before you choose one.

The Verbs *Has*, *Have*, and *Had*

Read the poem.

What If?

A cat has four.
A bird has two.
If snakes had these,
What could they do?

A worm has none.
A bee has two.
If you had these,
What could you do?

Dolphins have them.
Whales do, too.
If we had these,
What could we do?

Kathryn Corbett

Talk with a partner about the answers to the poem's riddles. Then talk about things animals have that you do not have. What do those things help animals do?

> Some verbs do not show action. They show that something belongs to someone.
>
> I **have** a book about elephants.
> The book **has** many pictures.
> I **had** a toy elephant once.

Work in a group to finish these sentences. Try to write a different thing for each animal.

A rabbit has _____.

A dog has _____.

A frog has _____.

A fish has _____.

Seals have _____.

Chickens have _____.

Porcupines have _____.

209

Using *Has*, *Have*, and *Had*

The verbs **has** and **have** tell about now.
Use **has** to tell about one.

> The snake **has** smooth skin.

Use **have** to tell about more than one.

> Snakes **have** long bodies.

The verb **had** tells about the past.

> Weeks ago the snake **had** green skin.
> The snakes **had** a smaller cage last year.

Guided Practice

Write *has*, *have*, or *had* to complete each sentence.

1. Today we _____ a snake.

2. Pat _____ a box for the snake now.

3. Most snakes _____ thin, pointy tongues.

4. Last week we _____ a turtle in the box.

5. Yesterday the turtle _____ a good meal.

Independent Practice

Write *has*, *have*, or *had* to complete each sentence.

6. Martha now _____ many pets.

7. Her birds _____ colorful feathers.

8. The rabbits _____ white fur.

9. Each pet _____ its own food today.

10. The animals now _____ cages.

11. Martha _____ a lot of work each day.

12. She _____ a busy day yesterday.

13. Yesterday the rabbits _____ a messy cage.

14. Today they _____ a clean cage.

15. Now the rabbits _____ a nice home.

Writing Connection

Recording Information Draw an animal you have or would like to have as a pet. Write a list of what you know about the animal. Tell what it looks like. Tell about its home. Use *has*, *have*, and *had* correctly.

You can use a computer drawing program to make a picture of the pet.

Agreement with *Has, Have,* and *Had*

Choose the form of *have* that agrees with, or goes with, the naming part of a sentence.

Pronoun	Now	The Past
I, you, we, they	have	had
he, she, it	has	had

Use *has* when the naming part tells about one. Use *have* with *I* and *you* and to tell about more than one. Use *had* to tell about the past.

Guided Practice

Decide if *have*, *has*, or *had* is used correctly. Write the incorrect sentences correctly.

1. Yesterday Tami has plans to go swimming.

2. Yesterday she had her swimsuit on.

3. Yesterday her friends had flippers.

4. Today Tami had a mask.

5. Now her friends had snorkels, too.

Remember Choose the form of *have* that agrees with, or goes with, the naming part of the sentence.

Independent Practice

Decide if *have*, *has*, or *had* is used correctly. Write the incorrect sentences correctly.

6. The ocean has many animals.

7. Now I had pictures of the ocean.

8. You had time to look at them now.

9. The dolphin in the picture has little teeth.

10. That fish has stripes.

11. I had a fish tank now.

12. Last year it has five fish in it.

13. Now the tank has only three fish.

14. That starfish has five arms.

15. Last summer I have a starfish, too.

Writing Connection

Revising Choose a piece of writing from your Writing Portfolio. Check to see whether you have used *have*, *has*, and *had* correctly. Revise any sentences that need changing.

Use your computer's grammar checker to look for sentences in which *have*, *has*, or *had* is used incorrectly.

Extra Practice

Write *has*, *have*, or *had* to complete each sentence.

1. We _____ a pond near our house.

2. Today the pond _____ frogs in it.

3. A frog _____ four legs.

4. Frogs _____ lungs for breathing air.

5. Two months ago, the pond _____ tadpoles in it.

6. Those tadpoles _____ tiny legs.

Decide if *have*, *has*, or *had* is used correctly. Write the incorrect sentences correctly.

7. Now the pond near our house had rocks by it.

8. Last night the rocks have salamanders on them.

9. I saw a salamander that have spots.

10. The pond always has many animals near it.

Language Play

How Many Do I Have?

- Play this game with a few other players.
- The first player hides some counters in a fist. Then the player asks the other players, "How many do I have?"
- The player whose guess is closest then takes a turn at hiding the counters.
- After all the players have had one turn, talk about the number of counters they had. Who had the most? Who had the fewest? Make sure you use *have, has,* and *had* correctly.

Writing Connection

Time Line A time line shows things that have happened over time. Make a time line of your life. Use this time line as a model.

I was born.		I went to preschool. I had new friends.		I am in second grade. I have Mr. Ting for my teacher. I have many friends.
1994	1996	1998	2000	2001
	Timmy, my little brother, was born.		I had chicken pox!	

Chapter Review STANDARDIZED TEST PREP

Choose the best answer for each underlined word.

1. Yesterday the owl <u>had</u> a hurt wing.

   a. have

   b. has

   c. correct as is

2. At that time, its wing <u>has</u> dirt on it.

   a. have

   b. had

   c. correct as is

3. Now the owl <u>have</u> a clean, mended wing.

   a. has

   b. had

   c. correct as is

4. We <u>have</u> other animals in the shelter today.

   a. had

   b. has

   c. correct as is

5. The animals <u>had</u> a good vet now.

   a. has

   b. have

   c. correct as is

6. Today the vet <u>had</u> a busy day ahead of her.

   a. has

   b. have

   c. correct as is

 Visit our website for more activities with *has*, *have*, and *had*.

www.harcourtschool.com

▣ Technology ▣

Editing on a Computer

A word processing program can help you revise and edit your writing and organize notes. You can use it to move words from one place in a document to another. To move words, you need to highlight them. Cut or Copy them, and then Paste them in the new place.

Practice

Type these notes on your computer. Then move the words to put them in a better order. Add numbers and any other words you need. Some parts are done for you.

Notes

gets bigger, taller
body grows, changes
gets stronger, heavier

adult   child
teenager   baby

people grow, change

Document 1

1. The body grows and changes.
   • gets bigger and taller
   •

2. People grow and change.
   • baby
   •
   •
   •

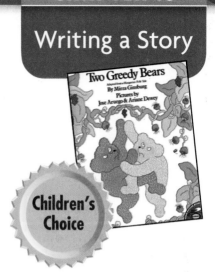

Children's
Choice

What makes a good story? Most good stories have strong characters, an interesting problem to solve, and a good ending. Think about these ideas as you read this story.

Two Greedy Bears

adapted from a Hungarian folk tale
by Mirra Ginsburg
pictures by Jose Aruego and Ariane Dewey

Two bear cubs went out to see the world. They walked and walked, until they came to a brook.

"I'm thirsty," said one.

"I'm thirstier," said the other. They put their heads down to the water and drank.

"You had more," cried one, and drank some more.

"Now you had more," cried the other, and drank some more. So they drank and drank, and their stomachs got bigger and bigger, until a frog peeked out of the water and laughed.

"Look at those pot-bellied bear cubs! If they drink any more they'll burst!"

The bear cubs sat down on the grass and looked at their stomachs.

"I have a stomach ache," one cried.

"I have a bigger one," cried the other. They cried and cried, until they fell asleep.

In the morning they woke up feeling better and continued their journey.

"I am hungry," said one.

"I am hungrier," said the other.

Suddenly they saw a big round cheese lying by the roadside. They wanted to divide it, but they did not know how to break it into equal parts. Each was afraid the other would get the bigger piece.

They argued, and they growled, and they began to
fight, until a fox came by.

"What are you arguing about?" the sly one asked
the bear cubs.

"We don't know how to divide the cheese so that
we'll both get equal parts."

"That's easy," she said. "I'll help you." She took the
cheese and broke it in two. She made sure that one
piece was bigger than the other, and the bear cubs
cried, "That one is bigger!"

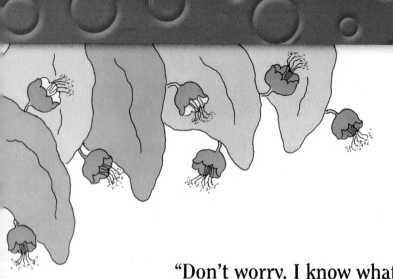

"Don't worry. I know what to do." She took a big bite out of the larger piece.

"Now that one's bigger!"

"Have patience!" She took a bite out of the second piece.

"Now this one's bigger!"

"Wait, wait," the fox said with her mouth full of cheese. "In just a moment they'll be equal." She took another bite, and then another.

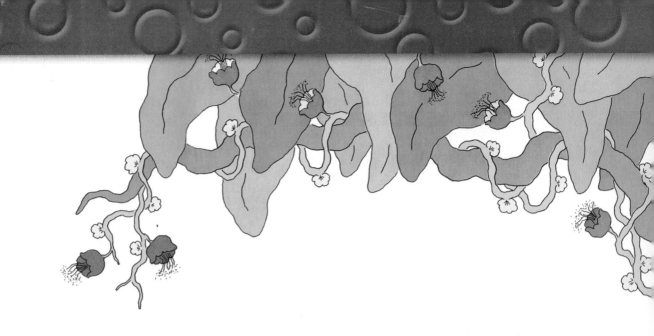

The bear cubs kept turning their black noses from the bigger piece to the smaller one, from the smaller one to the bigger one.

"Now this one's bigger!"

"Now that one's bigger!"

The fox kept on dividing and dividing the cheese, until she could eat no more.

"Now, good appetite to you, my friends!" She flicked her tail and stalked away.

By then all that was left of the big round cheese
were two tiny crumbs . . .
but they were equal!

Think About It

1. Which part of the story do you like best? Read it to a partner.

2. Why do the bear cubs drink so much water? How do you know? Why does the fox eat almost all the cheese at the end?

Parts of a Story

A good story has a **beginning**, a **middle**, and an **ending**.

The people or animals in the story are its **characters**.

The **setting** is when and where the story takes place.

On a sheet of paper, complete the story map for "Two Greedy Bears."

Beginning

Who?

When and where?

What is the problem?

Middle

What do the characters do to solve the problem?

Ending

How is the problem solved?

A Student Model

Pam liked reading the story about the two bear cubs. She wrote a story, too. Read Pam's story about puppies, and think about its parts.

Clancy's Bone

One morning Clancy woke up to find a big, juicy bone in his bowl. He quickly dug a hole and buried the bone. Later that day Clancy went to dig up his bone. When he got there, he saw that it was gone. His friend Nancy was chewing on his bone.

Clancy said, "Grr! Give me back my bone." He pulled on one end of the bone.

Nancy said, "Grr! It's my bone. I found it!" She pulled on the other end of the bone.

Clancy and Nancy pulled and pulled until they got tired. Then a big, mean dog came by and stole the bone. Clancy and Nancy decided never to fight over bones again.

The **title** gives a hint about what the story is about.

The **beginning** tells who the story characters are and what the problem is.

The **middle** tells how the characters try to solve the problem.

The **ending** tells how the problem is solved.

Dialogue helps show what the characters are like.

Looking at the Model

1. What is the title of Pam's story?

2. Who are the main characters?

3. What is the problem?

4. Who is another important character in the story? How does that character help solve the problem?

5. What do Clancy and Nancy decide at the end of the story?

Writer's Craft

Quotations That Show Feeling

Pam used dialogue to help you know what the characters are like. Find the dialogue in Pam's story.

- What does Clancy say?

- What does Nancy say?

- Why do you think the dogs are growling? How are they feeling?

- How do their words help you know these things?

Prewriting

Before Pam wrote her story, she made a list of characters and problems they might have. She wrote and drew her ideas.

Pam thought about her classmates who would read the story. She knows they like puppies. So she decided to write about puppies fighting over a bone. Then Pam filled in this story map to put her ideas in order.

Beginning

Who? two puppies

When and where? now, in a yard

What is the problem? The dogs both want to chew on the bone.

Middle

What do the characters do to solve the problem? They both pull at the bone without letting go.

Ending

How is the problem solved? A bigger dog comes by and steals the bone.

Your Turn

STEP 1 **Think of story ideas.**

Make a list of interesting characters and the problems they might have. Write or draw story ideas.

STEP 2 **Choose a story idea.**

Choose an interesting character and problem.

STEP 3 **Complete a story map.**

What Good Writers Do

✓ Remember for whom you are writing and why.

✓ Make a plan.

Beginning

Who?

When and where?

What is the problem?

Middle

What do the characters do to solve the problem?

Ending

How is the problem solved?

Drafting

Pam used the ideas in her story map to write the first draft of her story. A first **draft** is a first try. She wrote quickly to get all her ideas down. She knew she could fix any mistakes later.

Clancy's Bone

Clancy woke up to find a big, juicy bone in his bowl. He quickly dug a hole and buried the bone. Clancy went to get his bone. When he got there, he saw that it was gone. His friend was chewing on his bone.

Clancy said, Grr! Give me back my bone. He pulled on one end of the bone.

Clancy and Nancy pulled and pulled until they got tired. Then a big, mean dog came by

Look at how Pam's story follows her story map so far. What else might Pam write?

Beginning

Who? two puppies

When and where? now, in a yard

What is the problem? The dogs both want to chew on the bone.

Middle

What do the characters do to solve the problem? They both pull at the bone without letting go.

Ending

How is the problem solved? A bigger dog comes by and steals the bone.

What Good Writers Do

☑ Remember for whom you are writing and why.

☑ Don't worry about mistakes as you write. You can fix them later.

Y**🙂ur** Turn

Use your story map and What Good Writers Do to write a draft of your story.

Write your draft on a computer. Fix any mistakes later.

Revising

Pam read her draft to a few classmates. They talked about ways to make it better. See how Pam chose to revise her story.

DRAFT

Clancy's Bone

One morning
∧Clancy woke up to find a big, juicy bone in his bowl. He quickly dug a hole and buried the
Later that day   dig up
bone. ∧Clancy went to get his bone. When he got there, he saw that it was gone. His friend
Nancy
∧was chewing on his bone.

Clancy said, Grr! Give me back my bone. He pulled on one end of the bone.
Nancy said, "Grr! It's my bone. I found it!" She pulled on the other end of the bone.
∧Clancy and Nancy pulled and pulled until they got tired. Then a big, mean dog came by and stole the bbone. Clancy and nancy decided never to fight over bones again

Your Turn

Read your story to a small group. Talk about ways to make it better. Use What Good Writers Do and the Editor's Marks to make changes.

Proofreading

Pam read her story again to look for any mistakes. Why do you think Pam made each change in red?

DRAFT

Clancy's Bone

One morning
Clancy woke up to find a big, juicy bone in his bowl. He quickly dug a hole and buried the

Later that day   dig up
bone. Clancy went to get his bone. When he got there, he saw that it was gone. His friend

Nancy
was chewing on his bone.

Clancy said, "Grr! Give me back my bone." He pulled on one end of the bone.

Nancy said, "Grr! It's my bone. I found it!" She pulled on the other end of the bone.

Clancy and Nancy pulled and pulled until they got tired. Then a big, mean dog came by and

bone
stole the bbone. Clancy and nancy decided never to fight over bones again.

Your Turn

Now read your story again. Use What Good Writers Do and the Editor's Marks to fix any mistakes.

You can revise and proofread your draft on a computer.

233

Publishing

Pam wrote a final draft of her story. Later she added pictures and made her story into a little book to share with her classmates.

Your Turn

Write your story again neatly on a clean sheet of paper. Make the changes. Use a computer if you want. Here are some other fun publishing ideas to make your story special.

- **Make a shape book.**
  Write your story on a paper cutout shaped like one of your story characters.

- **Make a three-fold story.**
  Fold a big sheet of paper into three parts. Write the beginning, the middle, and the ending on the three parts. Draw a picture for each part.

Add your finished story to your Writing Portfolio.

Clancy's Bone

One morning Clancy woke up to find a big, juicy bone in his bowl. He quickly dug a hole and buried the bone. Later that day Clancy went to dig up his bone. When he got there, he saw that it was gone. His friend Nancy was chewing on his bone.

Clancy said, "Grr! Give me back my bone." He pulled on one end of the bone.

Nancy said, "Grr! It's my bone. I found it!" She pulled on the other end of the bone.

Clancy and Nancy pulled and pulled until they got tired. Then a big, mean dog came by and stole the bone. Clancy and Nancy decided never to fight over bones again.

Clancy's Bone

One morning Clancy woke up to find a big, juicy bone in his bowl. He quickly dug a hole and buried the bone. Later that day Clancy went to dig up his bone. When he got there, he saw that it was gone. His friend Nancy was chewing on his bone.

Clancy said, "Grr! Give me back my bone." He pulled on one end of the bone. Nancy said, "Grr! It's my bone. I found it!" She pulled on the other end of the bone.

Clancy and Nancy pulled and pulled until they got tired. Then a big, mean dog came by and stole the bone. Clancy and Nancy decided never to fight over bones again.

Listening and Speaking

Telling a Story

A good story can be written, but many good stories can be told. Think about how you could tell a story to others. Try one tip.

Storytelling Tips

- Make a puppet for each character. Use the puppets to act out the story.

- Use props and costumes to make the story events and characters come to life.

- Use different voices for different characters.

It is important to be a good listener when someone tells a story. Practice these tips.

Listening Tips

- Listen to find out what problem the character is trying to solve. Think about what happens in the beginning, middle, and ending.

- Listen to the details. Details help you understand what the characters are doing and feeling.

Adding *s* or *es* to Verbs pages 172–173

Write the correct verb to finish each sentence

1. Many animals (live, lives) in our pond.
2. Our dog (chase, chases) the frogs.
3. He never (catch, catches) them though.

Combining Sentences with Verbs pages 174–175

Use *and* to combine each pair of sentences. Write the new sentence.

4. Ben sits on a log.
   Ben watches a turtle.

5. The turtle digs a hole.
   The turtle lays its eggs.

Adding *ed* to Verbs pages 182–183

Rewrite each sentence. Change the verb to tell about the past.

6. We walk around the pond.
7. I climb on a huge rock.
8. Ben and I fish for a while.
9. We toss back the fish.

Changing Verbs That End with *e* pages 184–185

Write the verb in ( ) to tell about the past.

10. I (poke) a log.
11. Something (move)!
12. A water snake (surprise) us.

Using *Am*, *Is*, and *Are* pages 200–201
Write *am*, *is*, or *are* to finish each sentence.

13. Some snakes _____ not dangerous.

14. That snake _____ dangerous.

15. Ben _____ not afraid now.

Using *Was* and *Were* pages 202–203
Write *was* or *were* to finish each sentence.

16. We _____ at the pond all day.

17. The frogs _____ fun to watch.

18. I _____ glad to see a heron.

Using *Has*, *Have*, and *Had* pages 210–211
Write *has*, *have*, or *had* to finish each sentence.

19. I _____ my fishing pole yesterday.

20. Ben _____ my pole now.

21. Do you and your friends _____ fishing poles?

Agreement with *Has*, *Have*, and *Had* pages 212–213
Decide if the underlined verb is used correctly. Write each incorrect sentence correctly.

22. Our pond <u>has</u> many animals.

23. Last year we <u>have</u> one heron.

24. Now we <u>has</u> five herons.

Science

Weather Watcher

What is the weather like where you live? How does it change each day? Work together with classmates to watch and report on the weather.

Set Up a Weather Station

• Find a good place outside for your weather station.

• Get a thermometer. Make a rain gauge and a wind vane.

Observe and Record the Weather

• Go outside at the same time each day.

• Look at the sky. Is it cloudy, sunny, or both?

• What is the temperature? Read the thermometer to find out.

• Find out in what direction the wind is blowing. Use the wind vane.

• Check the rain gauge. Has it rained or snowed? How much?

• Write your weather notes in a log.

Make Daily Weather Reports

- Use your weather notes to prepare a weather report each day.

- Talk to your classmates about the weather. Watch television weather reports to get ideas for your talk.

- Write a weather report to put up in the classroom. Draw pictures to go with your report. Use a computer if you wish.

- Use e-mail to send weather reports to teachers, parents, and other people where you live.

Books to Read

Weather Words and What They Mean
by Gail Gibbons

Nonfiction
This book tells about weather words such as *temperature*, *thunderstorm*, and *moisture*.
Award-Winning Author

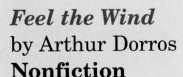

Feel the Wind
by Arthur Dorros
Nonfiction
Find out how the wind affects the Earth and how we use it to help us.
Outstanding Science Trade Book

Unit 4

Grammar
- All About Adjectives

Writing
- Poem
- Paragraph That Describes

Snowflakes

Snowflakes are like feathers
but smaller.
Snowflakes are like soap flakes
but wetter.
Snowflakes are like raindrops
but colder.
Snowflakes are like confetti
but icier.
Snowflakes are like tiny stars
falling quietly at night.

What Is an Adjective?

Read this paragraph from the book
Red Riding Hood.

retold and illustrated by James Marshall

A long time ago in a simple cottage beside the deep, dark woods, there lived a pretty child called Red Riding Hood. She was kind and considerate, and everybody loved her.

Talk about Red Riding Hood. Tell what she is like. Then write words that describe her.

An **adjective** describes, or tells about, a noun.

Red Riding Hood lives in a **small** cottage. Her cape is **red**.

Write an adjective that describes each underlined noun.

1. Red Riding Hood has a <u>basket</u> of food.

2. The food is for her <u>grandmother</u>.

3. Red Riding Hood walks through the <u>woods</u>.

4. She picks <u>flowers</u> along the way.

5. Why is the <u>wolf</u> hiding behind the tree?

243

Adjectives That Tell What Kind

Adjectives describe nouns. Some adjectives describe **color** and **shape**. They tell *what kind*.

Who lives in the **white** cottage?
Look at the **square** windows.

Guided Practice

Choose an adjective from the box to complete each sentence. Write the new sentence.

flat	red	green	orange	crooked

1. The girl with the _____ cape lives there.

2. Do you see her _____ cat?

3. Does the cat have a _____ tail?

4. The cat sits on a _____ stump.

5. _____ grass is by the cat.

Independent Practice

Choose an adjective from the box to complete each sentence. Write the new sentence.

yellow	white	gray	black	green
pointed	round	straight	flat	purple

6. Look at these _____ flowers.

7. That flower has _____ petals.

8. Its center is _____.

9. Look how _____ the stems are!

10. Each leaf has a _____ tip.

11. The leaves are also _____.

12. I see a _____ squirrel.

13. It is in the tall _____ grass.

14. Do you see the _____ fur on its belly?

15. How _____ its eyes are!

Writing Connection

Writing a Description Draw a picture of a butterfly. Then write a paragraph about it. Use adjectives to tell about its color and shape.

You can use your computer to help you draw and color your picture.

Writing Longer Sentences

> Adjectives can make your writing more interesting. They give more information about nouns. Use adjectives to create better word pictures.
>
> I see a snake on that rock.
> I see a **black** snake on that **big flat** rock.

Guided Practice

Add adjectives to describe the noun or nouns in each sentence. Write the new sentence.

1. I put on my jacket with the pockets.

2. Dad and I walked down to the pond.

3. We saw flowers in the water.

4. I looked at the leaves.

5. Fish swam by us.

Independent Practice

Add adjectives to describe the noun or nouns in each sentence. Write the new sentence.

6. I stood on a rock.

7. I fed the ducks.

8. Dad pointed to a turtle.

9. It had marks on its shell.

10. I once saw a snake here.

11. Do all snakes have fangs?

12. Dad saw a spider.

13. A fly was in its web.

14. Then a butterfly landed on me!

15. It had spots on its wings.

Writing Connection

Revising Choose a piece of writing from your Writing Portfolio. Find the nouns in your sentences. Add adjectives to make your sentences more interesting.

Use your computer to revise your writing.

Extra Practice

Write the adjective in each sentence.

1. What a beautiful day it is!

2. Ben goes for a long walk.

3. He puts on his old boots.

4. The path is muddy.

Choose an adjective from the box to complete each sentence.

| long | yellow | round | black |
| straight | brown | flat | orange |

5. Ben jumps into a pile of _____ leaves.

6. Ben sees a small _____ rock.

7. He uses a _____ stick to lift the rock.

8. Ben finds a _____ bug.

Add adjectives to describe the noun in each sentence. Write the new sentence.

9. Ben sees a deer.

10. It has spots.

Language Play

Adjective Trail

- Sit in a circle with a few classmates.
- Say a sentence about an animal. Put one adjective in your sentence.
- The next person adds one more adjective and says the new sentence.
- Go around the circle until each person has added an adjective. Write the whole sentence.
- Draw a picture to go with the sentence.

Use these sentences to get started. Don't forget to add an adjective.

I saw a _____ frog.

Look at the _____ snake!

He has a _____ dog.

Writing Connection

Riddle Fun Think of an object, and list adjectives to tell about its color and shape. Then use the adjectives to write a riddle on one side of a card. Write the answer on the back. Read the riddle to a classmate.

I can be any color.
I am made of wax.
I can write.

A crayon.

Chapter Review

STANDARDIZED TEST PREP

Find the adjective in each sentence. Choose the answer that shows that adjective.

1. I see a brown spider.

   a. I

   b. see

   c. brown

2. Its body is round.

   a. body

   b. round

   c. Its

3. The spider has pointed fangs.

   a. pointed

   b. fangs

   c. has

4. The spider's web looks like white thread.

   a. web

   b. thread

   c. white

5. A green bug is in a web.

   a. green

   b. bug

   c. web

6. It wiggles its small body.

   a. body

   b. small

   c. wiggles

Add adjectives to the sentences. Write the new sentences.

7. A spider makes a web.

8. The spider has legs.

▣ Study Skills ▣

Using a Thesaurus

A **thesaurus** is a list of words in alphabetical order. Each word in a thesaurus is called an **entry word**. The thesaurus lists synonyms for each entry word. A **synonym** is a word that means the same or almost the same as another word. Sometimes a thesaurus lists **antonyms**, or opposites, too.

Practice

Use the Thesaurus at the back of your book to answer each question.

1. On what page can you find the entry word *pretty*?

2. Does the word *pretty* come before or after the word *nice*?

3. What words mean almost the same as *pretty*?

4. What words are opposites for *pretty*?

5. What entry word comes after *pretty*?

Words That Tell About the Senses

Read the poem.

August Afternoon

Where shall we go?
What shall we play?
What shall we do
On a hot summer day?

We'll sit in the swing.
Go low. Go high.
And drink lemonade
Till the glass is dry.

One straw for you,
One straw for me,
In the cool green shade
Of the walnut tree.

Marion Edey

What are the adjectives the poet uses in "August Afternoon"? What do you hear, feel, smell, and taste during your favorite month? Talk with a partner. Write down the adjectives you use.

Some adjectives tell about the senses.

What shall we do on a **hot** summer day?
We will listen to the **noisy** birds.
We will drink **sweet** lemonade.

Write an adjective that describes each underlined noun.

Warm <u>Weather</u>

What shall we do today?

We will drink _____ <u>lemonade</u>

and listen to the _____ <u>bees</u> .

We will sit on a _____ <u>bench</u>

and eat_____ <u>fruit</u>

in the _____ <u>shade</u>

of the _____ <u>tree</u> .

Adjectives for Taste, Smell, Feel, and Sound

Some adjectives tell how something tastes, smells, feels, or sounds.

> We pick some **sweet** blueberries.
> The air smells **fresh**.
> We sit on a **bumpy** log.
> I listen to the **noisy** birds.

Guided Practice

Write a word from the box to complete each sentence.

noisy	warm	quiet	firm	sticky

1. The forest is _____.

2. It is a _____ day.

3. Three rangers walk on the _____ ground.

4. They hear some _____ bees.

5. The rangers see a hive filled with _____ honey.

Independent Practice

Write a word from the box to complete each sentence.

cool	crunchy	fresh	hard	quiet
slippery	soft	bitter	sticky	tasty

6. The rangers now walk on _____ rocks.

7. A rock falls and scares a _____ rabbit.

8. The rangers find a plant with a _____ smell.

9. The plant has _____ leaves and berries.

10. The rangers pick some _____ berries.

11. They put the fruit in a _____ bag.

12. Back home the rangers keep the bag in a _____ place.

Writing Connection

Write a Description Think about a fruit you like. Draw a picture of it. Then write sentences that tell how it tastes, smells, feels, and sounds when you eat it.

You can use a computer to print out your sentences.

Using Synonyms in Writing

A **synonym** is a word that means the same or almost the same as another word. Some synonyms are adjectives.

The birds in the forest are **loud**.
The birds in the forest are **noisy**.

Choose the synonyms to tell exactly what you mean to say.

I like to eat **tasty** blueberries.
I like to eat **sweet** blueberries.

The adjective *sweet* gives a better idea of how the blueberries taste.

Guided Practice

Choose the more exact adjective to finish each sentence.

1. The (rainy, wet) weather ends.

2. Water falls from the (bent, droopy) tree branches.

3. I sit on a (soggy, wet) log.

4. My dad gives me a (hot, spicy) sandwich.

5. It has some (crunchy, hard) carrots in it.

Independent Practice

Choose the more exact adjective to finish each sentence.

6. My father gives me some (sweet, tasty) berries to eat.

7. I drink some (cool, icy) water.

8. I pick up a (silky, soft) leaf.

9. A (cold, chilly) wind blows.

10. (Big, Huge) raindrops fall again.

11. I slip on a (slimy, wet) rock.

12. My foot touches a (soft, furry) thing.

13. It is a (fuzzy, hairy) chipmunk.

14. The chipmunk has (sparkly, bright) eyes.

15. It hides under a (rough, bumpy) root.

Writing Connection

Revising Choose a piece of writing from your Writing Portfolio. Check to see which adjectives you can replace with more exact synonyms.

Use your computer's thesaurus to help you find more synonyms.

Extra Practice

Write the adjective in each sentence.

1. The squirrel has soft fur.

2. I watch it eat hard nuts.

3. It climbs the bumpy branches.

4. It has a warm nest in a tree.

5. The quiet squirrel sleeps.

Write a word from the box to complete each sentence.

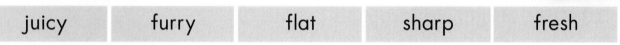

| juicy | furry | flat | sharp | fresh |

6. I sit on a _____ log and watch a squirrel.

7. It has a _____ tail.

8. It also has _____ teeth.

9. The squirrel bites into a _____ berry.

10. It sniffs the _____ air.

Choose the more exact synonym.

11. I have a (bright, shiny) apple.

12. I see a (little, tiny) animal.

13. The animal wants my (sweet, tasty) apple.

14. It has (black, dark) fur.

15. I gave it a (hard, crisp) piece of apple.

Language Play

Food Clues

- Take turns with a partner. Think of a food you like, but don't tell its name.
- Tell your partner how the food feels, tastes, and smells. You can also tell how it sounds when you eat it. Be sure to use exact adjectives.
- Have your partner guess the food.

Writing Connection

Write a Shape Poem Think about something you like, such as a flower or a fruit. Write a shape poem about it. Use adjectives to tell how it smells, feels, sounds, or tastes. Copy your poem onto a sheet of paper shaped like your topic.

Apples

I eat juicy apples.

I like crisp apples.

I bite crunchy apples.

An apple is a

great food!

Chapter Review

Choose the best synonym for each underlined adjective.

1. We ate some <u>tasty</u> blueberries.

    a. sweet

    b. spicy

    c. hard

    d. loud

2. Now we sit outside in the <u>cold</u> night.

    a. sharp

    b. sweet

    c. dull

    d. chilly

3. Our campfire has a <u>burnt</u> smell.

    a. smoky

    b. loud

    c. cool

    d. cold

4. We hear a <u>big</u> clap of thunder.

    a. tasty

    b. huge

    c. crunchy

    d. hot

5. <u>Cold</u> rain begins to fall on our camp.

    a. Sharp

    b. Smooth

    c. Icy

    d. Noisy

6. We all run into our <u>small</u> tents.

    a. tiny

    b. open

    c. big

    d. large

Visit our website for more activities with adjectives:
www.harcourtschool.com

◼ Vocabulary ◼

Antonyms   TAAS SKILL

> **Antonyms** are words that have opposite meanings.
>
> The campfire is **hot**.
> It is not **cold**.
>
> *Hot* and *cold* are antonyms.

Practice

Write an antonym from the box for each underlined adjective.

Antonyms			
dry wet	heavy light	soft hard	warm cool
good bad	large small	sweet sour	tall short

1. Many <u>large</u> plants grow in the forest.

2. I learned about one plant that grows in <u>wet</u> places.

3. This plant likes <u>cool</u> weather.

4. In spring its flowers smell <u>good</u>.

5. Then in summer its fruit is <u>sour</u>.

Using Colorful Words

Some poems have rhyming words. Some do not. Many poems have a **rhythm**, or beat, that makes them fun to read and hear.

Many poems "paint" word pictures with colorful words. **Colorful words** tell how something looks, feels, tastes, smells, or sounds.

Read this rhyming poem. Which words help you know what a squirrel is like?

Busy

Busy, busy, busy, busy,
Busy little squirrel—
Running, running, jumping,
In a dizzy whirl.
Stopping now and then to eat
A tasty little acorn treat—
Busy, busy, busy, busy,
Busy little squirrel.
                    Phyllis Halloran

*illustration by
Eric Carle*

Now read this poem that does not rhyme.
What are some of the colorful words? How
do they paint a word picture?

The Wind Is Cool and Swift

The wind is cool and swift.
The sea of colors is on the trees.
The mist of rain is soft and sweet.
The warmth of summer is gone.
Soon the land will be bare and gray.
I feel a warmth as the leaves change color.

Tanu Frank

Think About It

1. Which poem did you like better? Why?

2. How is the poem on this page like "Busy"?
How is it different?

Writer's Craft

Writing Colorful Words

Colorful words help readers know what something is like. Some of these words are adjectives. Some are action verbs.

Busy little squirrel— (adjectives)
Running, running, jumping, (action verbs)
In a **dizzy** whirl. (adjective)

The writer could have said that the squirrel runs around quickly. The word *dizzy* is more colorful, or interesting. It helps you picture just how the squirrel moves.

A. Write two colorful words to describe each word below. Use the Word Bank or your Thesaurus on page 494 to help you.

1. dog
2. fur
3. walks
4. tail
5. games
6. days
7. belly
8. food

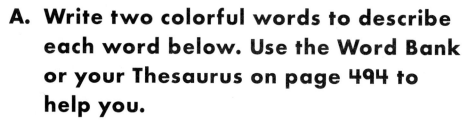

Word Bank	
chilly	fluffy
lazy	ragged
juicy	droopy
chummy	gloomy
sleepy	playful

B. Write a colorful word to complete each sentence in this poem that does not rhyme.

My Luna

My 1._____ dog is named Luna.

She has 2._____ fur.

She wags her 3._____ tail when I'm around.

Luna loves to play 4._____ games.

She has a 5._____ look in her eyes.

Luna 6._____ when I scratch her belly.

7._____ food makes Luna happy, too.

She and I both like 8._____ walks.

Luna 9._____ over the tall grass.

We have many 10._____ days together.

Writing and Thinking

Reflect Tell what helped you think of colorful words. Write your ideas. Share your ideas in a small group.

Applying the Craft TAAS SKILL

Read this student's poem. Think about how the underlined words paint a word picture.

Fuzzy Bunny

I have a little <u>fuzzy</u> bunny,

He thinks that carrots taste so <u>yummy</u>.

He's white and has a small black <u>spot</u>,

It looks just like a polka-<u>dot</u>.

He loves to <u>twitch</u> his <u>wet</u> pink nose,

All day long it goes and goes.

Sometimes I rub his <u>silky</u> tummy.

Isn't my little bunny funny?

Molly, age 7

colorful words

rhyming words

Looking at the Model

1. Which line in the poem do you think paints the best word picture? Why?

2. What do you notice about the words *nose* and *goes*? Why can words like these make the poem fun to read?

Your Turn

Write a poem for your classmates that tells about an animal or a place in nature.

Prewriting and Drafting

STEP 1 **Develop your ideas.**

Ask yourself these questions.

- What kinds of things does my audience like to read?
- Do I want my poem to rhyme?
- How can I use colorful words?

STEP 2 **Brainstorm colorful words.**

Make a web. Write colorful words that tell about your topic.

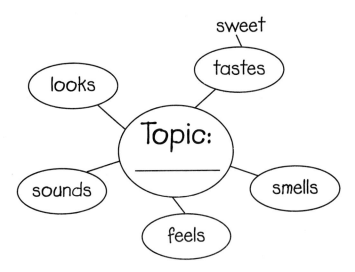

STEP 3 **Write your draft.**

Use your web and What Good Writers Do to write a draft of your poem.

What Good Writers Do

☑ Remember for whom you are writing and why.

☑ Plan your ideas.

Student Handbook

Use your Thesaurus to help you find colorful words.

Writer's Craft

Editing Your Poem

Share your draft with a few classmates. Together, talk about how you can make your poem better. Use the checklist and the Editor's Marks to help you revise your poem.

 My poem uses colorful words. The colorful words tell the reader what the topic is like.

 My poem has a title.

Editor's Marks	
∧	Add.
⋏	Change.
℘	Take out.
＝	Use a capital letter.
⊙	Add a period.
⬭	Check the spelling.

Sharing with Others

Meet with a partner or in a small group. Share your poem. Read it aloud.

Handwriting

Making Letters the Correct Size

Follow these tips to make sure your letters are the correct size.

- Tall letters touch the top line.
- All tail letters hang below the base line.
- Short letters touch the midline.

correct

April

incorrect

April

Write these letters. Use your best handwriting. Follow the tips to make your letters the correct size. Use the Handwriting Models on page 490 to help you.

tall letters   b   d   f   h   k   l

tail letters   g   j   p   q   y

short letters   a   c   e   i   m   n   o

r   s   u   v   w   x   z

Words for Size and Number

Read the poem.

The Cow

There's a cow on the mountain,
The old saying goes;
At the end of her legs
Are four feet and eight toes.
Her tail hangs behind
At the end of her back,
And her head sticks out front
At the end of her neck.

Chinese Mother Goose Rhyme

*illustration by
Ed Young*

With a partner, make a list of words from the poem that tell what the cow looks like. Then talk about an animal you like. Describe it. Tell about its size and things like legs, ears, and wings.

Some adjectives tell about size.

I see a **big** cow and a **small** calf.

Some adjectives tell how many.

The cow has **four** legs and **two** ears.

Think about an animal. It can be real or made up. Write its name on the first line of this new poem. Then write adjectives that tell about its size and body.

There is a _____ on the mountain.

At the end of _____ legs

are _____ feet and _____ toes.

A _____ head sticks out front

with _____ ears and _____ eyes

at the end of a _____ neck.

Adjectives That Tell How Many

Some adjectives tell how many. You can tell exactly how many with number words such as **one** and **two**.

The **four** children want breakfast.

You can tell about how many with words such as **few**, **some**, and **many**.

Dad will make **some** pancakes.

Guided Practice

Write the adjective that tells how many.

1. Cindy and Paul get one bag of flour.

2. They put two cups of flour in a bowl.

3. I add a few spoonfuls of water.

4. Jeff puts in three eggs.

5. Dad mixes the batter for ten seconds.

Independent Practice

Write the adjective that tells how many.

6. My two brothers hand Dad the frying pan.

7. Dad puts four drops of oil in the pan.

8. Then he pours in some of the batter.

9. It will make one pancake.

10. It takes two minutes to cook.

11. He makes many more.

12. Each person gets three pancakes.

13. Mom cuts four oranges into slices.

14. She puts some slices on each plate.

15. The breakfast will be ready in a few minutes.

Writing Connection

Functional Writing: Breakfast Menu

Imagine that you will make breakfast for your family. Think about how many people are in your family. Make a list of what you need. Use adjectives that tell how many.

- four eggs
- four pieces of toast
- some butter
- some jelly

Use your computer to help you write your menu.

273

Using *a* and *an*

A and **an** are special adjectives that mean "one." Use **a** before a word that begins with a consonant.

Astronauts ride in **a** space shuttle.

Use **an** before a word that begins with a vowel.

An adventure in space sounds like fun.

Guided Practice

Write *a* or *an* to complete each sentence.

1. I have always wanted to ride in _____ rocket.

2. First I will get _____ old box.

3. I will build _____ special rocket.

4. On one side of the box, I make _____ window.

5. Now I am _____ astronaut!

Independent Practice

Write *a* or *an* to complete each sentence.

6. I use _____ brush for a microphone.

7. _____ orange hat becomes my helmet.

8. I find _____ old shoe box.

9. The shoe box makes _____ good seat.

10. I use _____ skateboard for wheels.

11. I hear _____ engine roar.

12. It takes _____ minute to get into space.

13. I see _____ planet.

14. Isn't it _____ amazing sight?

15. _____ imaginary trip is fun!

Writing Connection

Revising Choose a piece of writing from your Writing Portfolio. Check whether you have used *a* and *an* correctly. Change words in your sentences, if you need to do so.

Use your computer to revise the sentences.

Extra Practice

Write an adjective from the box to complete each sentence.

1. _____ snowflakes fell on the lawn.

2. _____ inches of snow fell.

3. Jenny made _____ snowballs.

4. She aimed for the _____ tree on the hill.

5. She threw _____ snowball that hit the tree.

tiny
tall
three
four
one

Write the adjective that tells how many.

6. Jenny found many rocks for her snowman.

7. She used some rocks for buttons.

8. Two rocks made the eyes.

9. A few small rocks made the mouth.

10. One carrot was the nose.

Choose _a_ or _an_. Write the new sentence.

11. Jenny found (a, an) old sled.

12. Then she got (a, an) idea.

13. Her mom climbed (a, an) hill with her.

14. Jenny took (a, an) trip down on the sled.

15. Jenny had (a, an) fun time sledding.

Language Play

The Twelve Days of School

- Take turns with a classmate. Make up and add new lines to a song.
- Begin with these lines:
  On the **first** day of school
  my classmate gave to me
  one sharpened yellow pencil.
- Complete the ending of the next lines:
  On the **second** day of school
  my classmate gave to me, **two** _____.
- Keep going until you have made up lines for twelve days of school.

Writing Connection

Functional Writing: List of Materials Think about something you know how to make. Then think about what you need to make it. Write a list of things.

Paper-Plate Mask

- One paper plate
- One pair of scissors
- One pencil
- Some markers and crayons
- Two pieces of string

Chapter Review

STANDARDIZED
TEST PREP

**Choose the word that best completes
the sentence.**

1. We make ____ snow fort.

   a. some

   b. a

   c. large

2. ____ of my friends join me.

   a. Some

   b. Big

   c. Small

3. Yuri brings ____ iron
   shovel.

   a. many

   b. a

   c. an

4. We make a ____ pile
   of snow.

   a. few

   b. large

   c. five

5. ____ people add more snow.

   a. A

   b. Less

   c. Four

6. The fort is ____ .

   a. tall

   b. two

   c. a

**Visit our website for more
activities with adjectives:**

www.harcourtschool.com

◼ Technology ◼

Using Spell-Check

You can use spell-check on your computer to find words that are misspelled. The spell-check gives you a choice of words that could fix the misspelled word. You click on the correctly spelled word. The computer replaces the misspelled word for you.

Practice

Read each sentence. The misspelled word is underlined. Choose the correct spelling in ( ). You can use your computer's spell-check to check.

1. You can write a <u>storey</u>. (story, starry, store)

2. Write about clouds and <u>rane</u>. (ran, rain, rang)

3. Be <u>shure</u> to use a frog and fish. (share, shore, sure)

4. Give <u>yor</u> characters names. (your, or, you)

5. Draw a <u>pickture</u>, too. (picketer, picture, pick)

Words That Compare

Read the poem.

Spring Rain

The storm came up so very quick
    It couldn't have been quicker.
I should have brought my hat along,
    I should have brought my slicker.

My hair is wet, my feet are wet,
    I couldn't be much wetter.
I fell into a river once
    But this is even better.

Marchette Chute

Talk with a group about different kinds of weather. How are they alike? How are they different? Use adjectives, like *warmer*, to tell how weather can be different.

> You can use adjectives to **compare**.
>
> Summer rain can be **warmer** than spring rain.
>
> Winter rain is the **coldest** of all.

Add new lines to the poem. To finish each sentence, write an adjective that compares.

The rain came up so very **fast**.
  It couldn't have been _faster_.

The wind came up so very **strong**.
  It couldn't have been _____.

The fog came up so very **thick**.
  It couldn't have been _____.

My hair is damp, my feet are **damp**.
  I couldn't be much _____.

I walked in the **cold** snow once,
  but this is even _____!

Adding *er* and *est*

An adjective that ends with **er** compares two things.

A car is **fast**.
An airplane is **faster**.

An adjective that ends with **est** compares more than two things.

A jet is the **fastest** of the three.
A rocket is **fastest** of all.

Guided Practice

Write the correct form of the adjective in ( ) to finish each sentence.

1. This science fair is the (greater, greatest) of all.

2. Tina made her model (faster, fastest) than Jim did.

3. Her sea model is (deeper, deepest) than Jim's pond.

4. His model is much (smaller, smallest) than her model.

5. Aldo's steamboat is the (louder, loudest) thing of all.

Independent Practice

Write the correct form of the adjective in ( ) to finish each sentence.

6. Dana's ant farm has (fewer, fewest) ants than mine.

7. My ant farm is (newer, newest) than her farm.

8. Mario brought the (older, oldest) fossil of all.

9. It's the (smaller, smallest) of all the shells I have ever seen.

10. Sandy's recycled paper is (stronger, strongest) than cardboard.

11. It is also (darker, darkest) than cardboard.

12. This science fair is (greater, greatest) than the one we had last year.

Writing Connection

Colorful Adjectives Think about three things you find outside. Draw pictures and write sentences to compare them. Be sure to use colorful adjectives and to add *er* or *est* correctly.

Use your computer to write and revise your sentences.

Writing to Compare

You can use adjectives that compare to help tell how things are different from each other. This will give your readers a clear picture of the things you are comparing.

The children are looking for **large** rocks.
Ben found a rock that is **larger** than Jan's rock.
Sara found the **largest** rock of all.

Guided Practice

Read each item. Then add _er_ or _est_ to the adjective in dark letters to complete the second sentence.

1. Most of the rocks are **smooth.**

   My rock is _____ than Jeff's rock.

2. Some of the rocks are **dark.**

   Sam's rock is the _____ of all.

3. Jack and Lisa found **small** rocks.
   Lisa's rock is _____ than Jack's rock.

4. Maria, Tanya, and Rick found **round** rocks.
   Tanya's rock is the _____ of all.

Independent Practice

Read each item. Then add *er* or *est* to the adjective in dark letters to complete the second sentence.

5. Miss Lee had a **smart** idea for the rocks.
   The class had an even _____ idea.

6. Everyone made **small** rock animals.
   Who made the _____ one of all?

7. Dan made a **short** tail for his animal.
   Ann made a _____ tail than Dan did.

8. Beth, Lisa, and Al painted **bright** eyes.
   My rock animal has the _____ eyes of all.

9. Ed put **long** ears on his rock animal.
   Maria's had _____ ears than his.

10. Ted and Lisa painted **thick** stripes.
    Ted painted _____ stripes than Lisa did.

Writing Connection

Writing and Revising Draw three rock animals you might like to make. Write sentences to compare them.

Use your computer to check and revise your spelling.

Extra Practice

Write the adjective that compares in each sentence. Then circle the letters that were added.

1. Who painted the tallest tree?

2. Ann's tree is shorter than my tree.

3. This tree has fewer branches than that tree.

4. Sam's tree has the smallest leaves of all.

Write the correct form of the adjective in ( ) to finish each sentence.

5. Sue painted the (taller, tallest) buildings of all!

6. Max made a (higher, highest) mountain than Jill made.

7. Is the ocean (deeper, deepest) than the lake?

8. Jed made the (light, lightest) clouds of all.

Add *er* or *est* to the adjective in ( ). Then write the new sentence.

9. Mark painted the (bright) stars of all!

10. We made a (long) rainbow than the third graders made.

Language Play

Create a Group Story

- Write each word on an index card. Then put the cards in a pile.
- Cut six more index cards in half. Write **+ er** on half of the cards and **+ est** on the other half. Put these cards in another pile.
- Take turns with two or three players. The first player picks a card from each pile and says the adjective in a sentence. He or she uses it to start a story.
- The next player picks cards. He or she says a sentence to add to the story.

loud	small
long	short
tall	high
deep	smooth
sweet	dark
strong	smart

Writing Connection

Functional Writing: Shopper's Report Cut out pictures from ads for two items of clothing or toys you might buy. Compare the items. Which one is cheaper? Which one is bigger? Tell which one is better and why. Write a Shopper's Report like this one.

I want a new teddy bear. I saw two bears in a catalog. The brown bear has longer arms, brighter eyes, and softer fur than the blue bear. It is also cheaper. I think the brown bear is better.

Chapter Review

STANDARDIZED TEST PREP

Choose the word that correctly completes each sentence.

1. Dad planned the _____ tree house I've ever seen.

    a. great

    b. greater

    c. greatest

2. He buys the _____ wood of all at the lumberyard.

    a. strong

    b. stronger

    c. strongest

3. We need _____ nails than the ones we have at home.

    a. long

    b. longer

    c. longest

4. Dad chooses the _____ tree of all in our yard.

    a. old

    b. older

    c. oldest

5. Is this branch _____ than the other one?

    a. thick

    b. thicker

    c. thickest

6. Dad is a _____ worker than I am.

    a. fast

    b. faster

    c. fastest

Visit our website for more activities with adjectives that compare:

www.harcourtschool.com

▣ Study Skills ▣

Using Pictographs and Bar Graphs

Graphs make it easy to compare numbers of things. A **pictograph** uses pictures to show how many. A **key** tells you how many each picture stands for in the graph.

A **bar graph** also shows how many.

Pictograph

Books Read in October	
Tom	📖 📖 📖 📖
Ann	📖 📖 📖
Sam	📖 📖 📖 📖 📖
Beth	📖 📖 📖 📖
Key: 📖 = 1 book	

Bar Graph

Books Read in October					
Tom					
Ann					
Sam					
Beth					
	1	2	3	4	5

Practice

Use the graphs to answer the questions.

1. What do both graphs show?

2. How many children are shown on each graph?

3. How many books did Sam read?

4. Who read the fewest books?

5. Which graph do you think is easier to read? Why?

CHAPTER 24

Writing a Paragraph That Describes

A good description tells how things look, sound, smell, taste, and feel. Think about the words this writer uses.

PENGUINS!

BY GAIL GIBBONS

Award Winning Author and Illustrator

Here come the penguins, straight and tall. They walk with a waddle, yet look stately and dignified.

A penguin's many feathers are small and stiff.
They form a warm and waterproof covering. In
really cold places, penguins have an extra layer
of long, downy feathers underneath. They also
have thick layers of fat to keep them warm.

Some Kinds of Penguins

EMPEROR PENGUIN

MACARONI PENGUIN

KING PENGUIN

CHINSTRAP PENGUIN

LITTLE BLUE PENGUIN also called FAIRY PENGUIN

GENTOO PENGUIN

GALAPAGOS PENGUIN

There are seventeen different kinds of penguins. The smallest is the little blue penguin. It is about one foot (30 centimeters) tall. The biggest of all penguins is the emperor penguin, standing almost four feet (120 centimeters) tall.

ROCKHOPPER PENGUIN

Crest

MAGELLANIC PENGUIN

YELLOW-EYED PENGUIN

AFRICAN PENGUIN also called BLACK-FOOTED PENGUIN

ADELIE PENGUIN

Crown

Eye

Beak or Bill

Throat

Neck

Back

Breast

Belly

Wing

Legs

Tail

Webbed Feet

All penguins have black or bluish-gray backs and white bellies. The patterns around their necks and heads are what make them look different. Some have colorful patches. Others show off brightly colored crests. They all have the same basic body shape and characteristics.

Penguins are birds, but they lost their ability to fly millions of years ago. Over time they began to spend a lot of time hunting for food in frigid waters. Their wings changed into powerful, rigid flippers for swimming.

Penguins have sleek, smooth bodies that glide easily through the water. They are excellent swimmers and divers. Larger ones can swim faster than 25 miles (40 kilometers) an hour. The emperor penguin can dive deeper than any other bird, about 1,500 feet (450 meters).

NORTH POLE

SOUTH POLE

SOUTHERN HEMISPHERE

All penguins are found in the Southern Hemisphere.

Today penguins are in danger. Now there are laws to protect them. People work together to help penguins survive in our modern world.

Think About It

1. What do most penguins look like? Tell how they look when they walk and swim.

2. What was one of the most surprising things you learned about penguins?

Parts of a Paragraph That Describes

A paragraph that describes tells what something is like. It uses words that tell how the thing looks, sounds, feels, tastes, and smells. These words give a good word picture.

Like all good paragraphs, a paragraph that describes has a main-idea sentence and detail sentences. It is indented.

Read the paragraph on page 291 again. Use it to complete this web on a separate sheet of paper.

how they feel

how they look

a penguin's feathers

other details

A Student Model

TAAS SKILL

Sumi liked reading about penguins. She decided to write her own paragraph about cats. Read the paragraph to see its important parts.

Cats

Cats are beautiful animals in many ways. They have very soft, silky fur. Their fur may be gray, black, white, orange, or even striped. Cats smell cleaner than many other animals because they lick themselves to keep clean. Cats can also make different noises! They may meow when they are hungry or want you to pet them. When they are happy, they make a low, rumbling purr.

The **title** names the topic, or what the paragraph is about.

The **main idea** tells what the paragraph is about.

Details give examples to explain the main idea.

Looking at the Model

1. What is the title of Sumi's paragraph? Why do you think she chose that title?

2. What is the topic of Sumi's paragraph?

3. What is the main idea of her paragraph?

4. What does Sumi tell about the way cats look? What does she say about the way cats smell?

5. How do you think Sumi feels about cats? Why do you think so?

Writer's Craft

Using Colorful Words

Sumi wanted her paragraph to tell as much about cats as possible. She used colorful words to show her readers exactly why she likes cats. Find the parts of Sumi's paragraph that are the most colorful.

• What words does Sumi use to describe cats' fur?

• What do cats do when they are happy? What words does Sumi use to describe the way cats purr?

Writing a
Paragraph That
Describes

Prewriting

Sumi learned much from reading about penguins. Before Sumi wrote a paragraph to describe an animal, she made a list of animals and drew a picture of each one.

Next she talked over her list with some classmates. She found out that they really liked cats. Sumi liked cats, too.

Then Sumi looked in books about cats to give her more ideas and information. She wrote words in this web to describe cats.

cats

kangaroos

bears

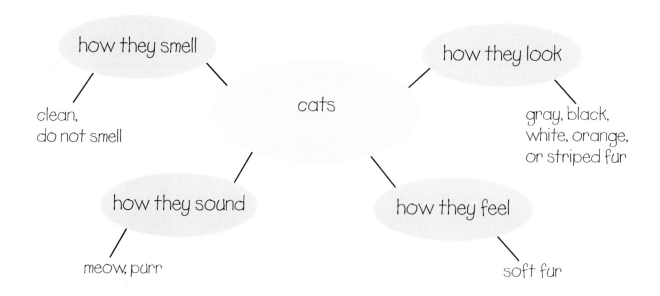

how they smell

clean,
do not smell

cats

how they look

gray, black,
white, orange,
or striped fur

how they sound

meow, purr

how they feel

soft fur

Your Turn

STEP 1 **Think of topics for your paragraph.** Make a list of things that you could describe. Draw or write your ideas.

STEP 2 **Choose a topic.** Talk about your list with classmates. Choose an idea that both you and they find interesting.

STEP 3 **Complete a word web.** Look through books and other resources to get more ideas and information. Then write words that describe your topic.

What Good Writers Do

✔ Think about for whom you are writing and why.

✔ Plan your writing.

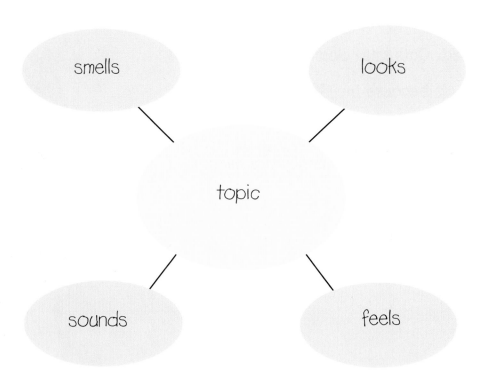

Drafting

Sumi used the details in her word web to
write a draft of her paragraph. She did not
worry about mistakes because she knew she
could make changes later.

Cats

Cats are nice animals. They have very soft,
fur. Their fur may be gray, black, white, or
even striped. Cats smell cleaner than many
other animals because they lick themselves
to keep clean. Cats can make different
noises! They may meow when they are hungry
or want you to pet them.

Read Sumi's first draft. Look over her word web. What might she write next?

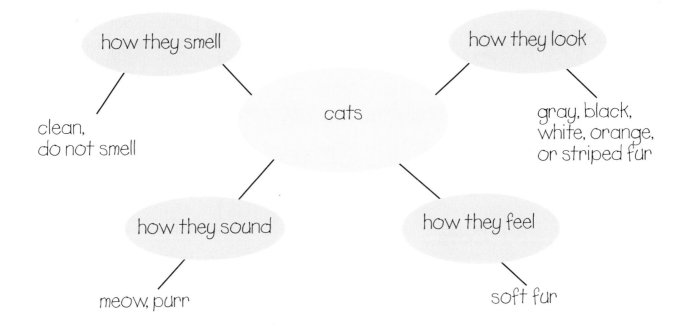

how they smell

clean, do not smell

cats

how they look

gray, black, white, orange, or striped fur

how they sound

meow, purr

how they feel

soft fur

What Good Writers Do

✓ Remember for whom you are writing and why.

✓ Describe your topic so that your readers can picture it.

✓ Use colorful adjectives to describe your topic clearly.

Y😊ur Turn

Use your word web and What Good Writers Do to write a draft of your paragraph that describes.

You can write your draft on a computer.

Revising

Sumi shared her draft with some classmates. They had ideas for ways to make it better. Read Sumi's revisions.

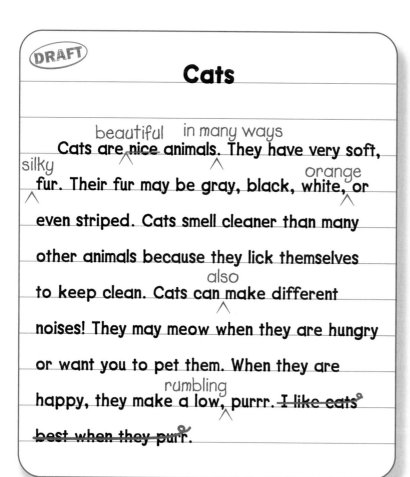

DRAFT

Cats

Cats are ~~nice~~ *beautiful* animals. *in many ways* They have very soft, *silky* fur. Their fur may be gray, black, white, *orange* or even striped. Cats smell cleaner than many other animals because they lick themselves to keep clean. Cats can *also* make different noises! They may meow when they are hungry or want you to pet them. When they are happy, they make a low, *rumbling* purrr. ~~I like cats best when they purr.~~

Your Turn

Now share your description with a partner. Ask him or her how it could be better. Use What Good Writers Do and the Editor's Marks to make changes.

Proofreading

Sumi read her paragraph one more time to check for mistakes. Think about why she made each change you see in red.

What Good Writers Do

✓ Make sure each sentence ends with the correct end mark.

✓ Make sure each word that compares is correct.

✓ Check spelling.

✓ Remember to leave margins.

DRAFT

Cats

Cats are ~~nice~~ beautiful animals ∧ in many ways. They have very soft, silky ∧ fur. Their fur may be gray, black, white, or orange ∧ even striped. Cats smell cleaner than many other animals because they lick themselves to keep clean. Cats can also ∧ make different noises! They may meow when they are hungry or want you to pet them. When they are happy, they make a low, rumbling ⟨purrr⟩ purr. ~~I like cats best when they purr.~~

Editor's Marks

= Use a capital letter.

∧ Add a comma.

◯ Check the spelling.

Your Turn

Read your paragraph again. Use What Good Writers Do and the Editor's Marks to fix any mistakes.

You can fix mistakes easily on a computer without typing a whole new paragraph.

Publishing

Sumi made a big cutout of a cat. Then she glued the final copy of her paragraph in the cutout.

Your Turn

Make a clean copy of your paragraph. Here are some other ideas for publishing your paragraph.

Cats

Cats are beautiful animals in many ways. They have soft, silky fur. Their fur may be gray, black, white, orange, or even striped. Cats smell cleaner than many other animals because they lick themselves to keep clean. Cats can also make different noises. They may meow when they are hungry or want you to pet them. When they are happy, they make a low, rumbling purr.

- **Turn your paragraph into an encyclopedia article.**

  Type your description on a computer. Add a heading and show how to pronounce the name. Include a picture of your topic. Make it all look like a page from an encyclopedia.

- **Make a sensory display.**

  Glue your paragraph on one side of a piece of posterboard. On the other side, draw a picture of the thing you describe. Add materials to show what the thing feels like. Make a tape recording of what the thing sounds like.

Add your final paragraph to your Writing Portfolio.

Listening and Speaking

Making Announcements

You can share information by making an announcement. An announcement is a speech you make to tell people about something.

Practice these tips.

Speaking Tips

- Plan your announcement. Make notes of important details, such as *who*, *what*, *where*, *when*, and *why*.

- First tell the main idea of your announcement. Then explain the details. Choose words to make your message clear.

- Use a loud, clear voice.

- Use hand movements to help you get your message across.

Listening Tips

- Listen to the whole announcement.
- Write notes about important details.
- If you are not sure about what you heard, give a short summary of what you understood. Then ask questions.

Unit 4
Grammar Review
pages 244–285

Adjectives That Tell What Kind pages 244–245
Choose an adjective from the box to complete each sentence. Write the sentence.

1. This apple is _____!
2. It is as _____ as a ball.
3. Some apples are _____.

round

green

red

Writing Longer Sentences pages 246–247
Add adjectives to describe the nouns in the sentences. Write each new sentence.

4. I see a butterfly.   5.   It has marks on its wings.

Adjectives for Taste, Smell, Feel, and Sound pages 254–255
Choose an adjective from the box to complete each sentence. Write the sentence.

6. Celery is a _____ vegetable.
7. It is full of _____ juice.
8. I love this _____ snack.

tasty

fresh

crunchy

Using Synonyms in Writing pages 256–257
Choose the more exact adjective to finish each sentence.

9. What animal has (soft, silky) fur?

10. Which one leaves a (slimy, wet) trail?

Adjectives That Tell How Many pages 272–273
Write the adjective that tells how many.

11. I picked three pints of blueberries.

12. We used two pints of berries for muffins.

13. We made many muffins and a small pie.

Using *a* and *an* pages 274–275
Write *a* or *an* to complete each sentence.

14. I made _____ bird feeder.

15. I used _____ empty milk jug.

Adding *er* and *est* pages 282–283
Write the correct form of the adjective in ( ) to finish each sentence.

16. A pumpkin is (larger, largest) than an orange.

17. A berry is the (smaller, smallest) of all three fruits.

Writing to Compare pages 284–285
Add *er* or *est* to the adjective in bold type to complete the sentence.

18. Lynn drew three tall birds. The ostrich is the **tall** one of all.

19. The eagle has short legs. The duck has **short** legs than the eagle.

Science

Literature

The Old and the New

Long ago, people wondered about things in nature. To explain these things, they made up stories. Today science explains many things in nature.

Read some of these stories. Read about how science explains the same things. Then show how they are all alike and how they are different.

Find and Read the Literature

- Look in the library.

- Decide what things in nature you want to read about. You may want to read about only one topic. For example, many stories are about why animals look and act the way they do.

- Read each story you chose. Then read it again and take notes.

Find and Read Science Facts

- Find science facts about your topic. Look in the reference and science sections of your library.

- Take notes on the science facts you find.

Show What You Have Learned

- Make a chart that tells how the stories and science facts are alike and how they are different.

- Give a talk. Describe the stories and the science facts. Then explain how they are alike and different. Use pictures to help you.

- Do a skit for each story. Then tell what really happens in nature.

Books to Read

Why the Sun and the Moon Live in the Sky
by Elphinstone Dayrell
Folktale
This African story tells how the sun and the moon came to be in the sky.
Caldecott Honor

The Acorn Tree and Other Folktales
by Anne Rockwell
Folktale
This book has ten stories from different parts of the world.
Award-Winning Author

Cumulative Review

Units 1–4

Unit 1: All About Sentences

Sentences pages 24–29, 36–37

Write each group of words in order to make a sentence. Circle the naming part. Underline the telling part.

1. the park Jack went to

2. next to his house the park is

3. he his friends meets to play

Kinds of Sentences pages 54–55, 64–65

Change each sentence to the kind of sentence in ( ). Write the new sentence.

4. This is your house. *(question)*

5. You have a nice room. *(exclamation)*

6. You should have a party. *(command)*

7. Can you invite your friends? *(statement)*

Unit 2: All About Nouns

Nouns pages 96–97

Write each sentence. Underline each noun. Write if it is a person, place, or thing.

8. Is there a sign on the corner?

9. Trees and swings are in the park.

10. My friend lives on my block.

Using Possessive Nouns pages 100–101

Use 's to rewrite the underlined words.

11. The computer of Ann is on the desk.

12. The baseball of my brother is missing.

13. Mike is looking for the flashlight of Dad.

Using *He, She, It,* and *They* pages 136–137

Write a pronoun for the underlined words.

14. My sister Amy has two dogs.

15. The two dogs play together.

16. My brother Jerry goes to the pet store.

17. The pet store is three blocks away.

Unit 3: Verbs

Using the Correct Verb pages 172–173, 202–203

Write the correct verb to finish each sentence.

18. The spider (spin, spins) its web.

19. The web (was, were) very beautiful.

20. The birds (build, builds) their nests.

21. The nests (was, were) very strong.

Adding *ed* to Verbs pages 182–183

Rewrite each sentence. Change the verb to tell about the past.

22. We walk along the path.

23. Two squirrels race up a tree.

24. Some deer leap across the meadow.

Write *has, have,* or *had* to finish each sentence.

25. Last year, I _____ a leaf collection.

26. My friend _____ my collection now.

27. Do you _____ a collection?

Unit 4: All About Adjectives

Adjectives pages 244–245, 254–255, 272–273

Choose an adjective from the box to complete each sentence. Write the sentence.

hard smooth two squeaky long loud

28. Spiders have _____ legs.

29. Snakes have _____ skin.

30. Birds have _____ wings.

31. Turtles have _____ shells.

32. Lions have a _____ roar.

33. Mice make _____ sounds.

Adding *er* and *est* pages 282–283

Write the correct form of the adjective in ( ).

34. An elephant is (small, smaller) than a blue whale.

35. Blue whales are the (longer, longest) of all the whales.

36. Giraffes are (taller, tallest) than elephants.

37. Cheetahs run the (faster, fastest) of all.

Standardized Test Prep

Making Nouns Plural pages 108–109

Write the correct noun that names more than one.

38. We sat on two _____.

   a. benches   **b.** benchs   **c.** bench

39. We ate four _____.

   a. sandwichs   **b.** sandwich   **c.** sandwiches

40. I saw two _____ running.

   a. fox   **b.** foxs   **c.** foxes

41. They ran behind two _____.

   a. rock   **b.** rocks   **c.** rockes

Using *Am*, *Is*, and *Are* pages 198–201

Write the correct verb for each sentence.

42. I _____ not afraid of insects.

   a. am   **b.** is   **c.** are

43. Some insects _____ colorful.

   a. am   **b.** is   **c.** are

44. That insect _____ scary.

   a. am   **b.** is   **c.** are

45. Spiders _____ not insects.

   a. am   **b.** is   **c.** are

Unit 5

Grammar
- More About Verbs

Writing
- Directions
- How-to Paragraph

Make a Photo Mobile

1. Get a hanger, paints, crayons, markers, yarn, paper, glue, a paper punch, and some photographs.

2. Glue the photographs onto different shapes of paper. Paint or color the borders.

3. Punch a hole at the top of each picture.

4. Use yarn to tie your pictures to the hanger. Hang up your mobile!

The Verbs *Come, Run,* and *Give*

Read the poem.

This Is My Rock

This is my rock,
And here I run
To steal the secret of the sun;

This is my rock,
And here come I
Before the night has swept the sky;

This is my rock,
This is the place
I meet the evening face to face.

David McCord

Tell why you think the rock is special to the poet. Then talk with a classmate about a place that is special to you.

The verbs **come**, **run**, and **give** tell about now. Add **s** to tell what one person, animal, or thing does. Do not add **s** when using **I**.

I **come** home.
The sun **comes** out now.
Ramon **runs** to Maria's house.
He **gives** her a drawing of the sun.

Write a poem like the one you just read. Write the name of your special place in the first line. Use the verbs come, run, and give in some of the other lines if you can.

319

Using *Come*, *Run*, and *Give*

The verbs **come**, **run**, and **give** tell about now.

> Today we **come** to the theater by bus.
> We **run** to the bus stop.
> We **give** our tickets to the bus driver.

The verbs **came**, **ran**, and **gave** tell about the past.

> Yesterday we **came** into the city by train.
> We **ran** to catch the train.
> We **gave** our tokens to the conductor.

Guided Practice

Write the correct verb in ( ) to complete each sentence.

1. I (come, came) to the museum today.

2. Last month my mom (give, gave) me some tickets.

3. She now (comes, came) to the museum to work.

4. Now she (gives, gave) me a tour of Dinosaur Hall.

5. I (run, ran) to see the dinosaurs right now!

Independent Practice

Write the correct verb in ( ) to complete each sentence.

6. Last week I (ran, run) to the museum.

7. My uncle (gave, give) me a free ticket.

8. Now I (come, came) to the museum again.

9. I walk in and (run, ran) to meet my uncle.

10. I greet him and (give, gave) him a hug.

11. Now we (run, ran) to the Dinosaur Hall.

12. My uncle (come, came) here to draw last weekend.

13. He (give, gave) me his drawings last Sunday.

14. Now he (gives, gave) me a pencil and some paper.

15. He (comes, came) with me now to draw a dinosaur.

Writing Connection

Telling About Now or About the Past
Think about an interesting place you visited. Write a few sentences about it. Use the verbs *come, run, give,* or *came, ran, gave.*

To print your sentences, you may be able to choose Print from the File menu.

Joining Sentences

You can use **and** to join two sentences that tell about the same thing. Add a **comma (,)** before **and** to separate the ideas.

The teacher set up the table for the art show.
The children sorted their drawings.

The teacher set up the table for the art show,
and the children sorted their drawings.

Guided Practice

Use *and* to join the sentences. Remember to use a *comma (,)* before *and*.

1. The clock said 9:00.
   People came to our show.

2. We were in the museum.
   People came to look at our art.

3. My parents walked in.
   I showed them my drawings.

4. The art teacher came by.
   My parents talked to her.

> 💡 **Remember** Use *and* to join two sentences that tell about the same thing. Put a *comma (,)* before *and*.

Independent Practice

Use *and* to join the sentences. Remember to use a *comma (,)* before *and*.

5. My teacher talked about my work.
   Dad thanked her.

6. Dad looked at more drawings.
   Mom took pictures of the show.

7. Diego showed his dinosaur poster to a girl.
   She liked it very much.

8. The director of the museum came by.
   I ran to say hello.

9. The director is also a teacher.
   I study art with him.

10. Many people came to the show.
    We were very proud.

Writing Connection

Revising Choose a story you like from your Writing Portfolio. Where can you join sentences? Revise your writing to make it more interesting.

To type a comma (,) using the computer, press ⎣,⎦ .

Extra Practice

Write the correct verb in ( ) to finish each sentence.

1. Last week my uncle (give, gave) me a note about a play.

2. Now I (come, came) to the play with my parents.

3. We (run, ran) now because we are late.

Change the verb in each sentence to tell what happened yesterday.

4. We come into the city.

5. We run to the theater.

6. My parents give money for the tickets.

Use *and* to join the sentences. Remember to use a *comma (,)* before *and*.

7. My uncle was in a play.
   I wanted to see him.

8. The play was about animals.
   My uncle played a lion.

9. I asked my parents if we could go.
   They got tickets.

10. My uncle was a great lion.
    It was fun to watch him.

324

Language Play

Sentence Time

- Use the game board below.
- Take turns with a partner. Roll a number cube.
- Find the matching number in the chart. Make up a sentence using the verb. Use the clue *today* or *yesterday* to know whether to change the verb.
- Keep playing until each player has used each word in a sentence.

	come	run	give
today	1	2	3
yesterday	4	5	6

Writing Connection

Making Lists Making lists can help you remember. Write sentences to list the things you often give to your friends and family. Then list what people have given you in the past. This list can help you remember to whom to write a thank-you note.

I give cards.
I give hugs.

Sue gave me a Valentine's Day card.

Tom gave me a book.

Chapter Review **STANDARDIZED TEST PREP**

Choose the best answer for each underlined word.

1. It was Thanksgiving, <u>and</u> all my family was there.

   a. It was Thanksgiving and, all my family was there.

   b. It was Thanksgiving And all my family was there.

   c. correct as is

2. My cousin Amy gave me a <u>book And</u> I smiled.

   a. My cousin Amy gave me a book, and I smiled.

   b. My cousin Amy gave me a book and, I smiled

   c. correct as is

3. She <u>come</u> to Thanksgiving dinner with her brother.

   a. Come

   b. came

   c. correct as is

4. Now she <u>come</u> for New Year's Eve.

   a. comes

   b. came

   c. correct as is

5. I <u>gave</u> her a card now.

   a. give

   b. gaves

   c. correct as is

6. Now she <u>ran</u> outside to show her brother.

   a. Ran

   b. runs

   c. correct as is

Visit our website for more activities with verbs:
www.harcourtschool.com

Study Skills

Using a Newspaper

A newspaper gives the news. It can tell what is happening around the world and in your town.

A newspaper tells about many subjects. It can tell what is happening in neighborhoods, sports, art, and the weather.

author —

The story tells *who, what, where, when,* and *why.*

Class Trip to the Museum —

by Bob Parker

The title of a news story is called a *headline.*

Yesterday, Mrs. Soto took a bus to Mapletown with her class. They all came to the museum to see the new Dinosaur Hall. The guide talked about the fossils and about how the dinosaurs lived. After the visit, the guide gave out pictures of dinosaurs.

Practice

Use the news story to answer the questions.

1. Who is the story about?

2. What did they do?

3. Where is the museum?

4. When did the class go there?

5. Why did they go to the museum?

CHAPTER 26

The Verbs *Go, Do,* and *See*

Read the poem.

Where I Went

I went up the high hill,
There I saw a climbing goat;
I went down by the running rill,
There I saw a ragged sheep;
I went out to the roaring sea,
There I saw a tossing boat;
I went under the green tree,
There I saw two doves asleep.

from The Mother Goose Treasury
by Raymond Briggs

Read the poem again with a partner. Then talk about where the poet went and what he saw.

The verbs **go**, **do**, and **see** tell about the present, or now.

> I **go** to the beach.
> I **do** a cartwheel in the sand.
> I **see** a boat on the water.

The verbs **went**, **did**, and **saw** tell about the past.

> I **went** to the lake.
> I **did** some swimming.
> I **saw** two frogs jumping.

Think about places you have gone and what you saw there. Then write an ending to each sentence to add new lines to the poem.

I went to the park.

There I saw a leaping squirrel.

I _____.
There I _____.
I _____.
There I _____.

Using *Go*, *Do*, and *See*

The verbs **go**, **do**, and **see** tell about now.

I **go** to art class today.   She **goes** with me.
I **do** a good job.   He **does** well, too.
I **see** other children.

The verbs are spelled **went**, **did**, and **saw** to tell about the past.

My sister **went** to a drawing class last week.
She **did** three drawings.
We **saw** her pictures.

Guided Practice

Choose the correct verb to finish each sentence.

1. Last week I (go, went) to a concert.

2. I (see, saw) a school band at the concert.

3. Now I (go, went) to music class.

4. I (see, saw) my teacher every day.

5. She says I always (do, did) a good job.

Independent Practice

Choose the correct verb to finish each sentence.

6. Right now my parents and I (go, went) into a concert hall.

7. Today we (see, saw) people play music.

8. We (do, did) this last month, too.

9. I (see, saw) a great guitar player last time.

10. He (do, did) some funny things.

11. Later I (see, saw) him play a toy guitar.

12. Now the guitar player (does, did) a song I love.

13. He (sees, saw) me and smiles at me.

14. The show is over, and we (go, went) backstage.

15. Now I (see, saw) the guitar player and thank him for the song.

Writing Connection

Sentences About an Experience Think about a time you went to a show. Write sentences about what you saw and did. Check your verbs.

Use a computer to type your sentences. Save your work.

Commas in Place Names and Dates

> Always use a **comma (,)** between the names of a city and a state.
>
> We went to **Dallas, Texas**.
>
> Always use a **comma (,)** between the day and the year in a date.
>
> My brother was born on **April 11, 1999.**

Guided Practice

Write the dates and the names of places correctly.

(1) March 16 2001

Dear Betty,
    We love the big city of
(2) Denver Colorado.
Yesterday we went to see a
play. It was very funny. We will
go to a concert in (3) Sedona
Arizona on (4) March 20 2001.

Your friend,
Jen

Betty Baker
10 James Street
(5) Ocean City Maryland 21842

Independent Practice

Write the dates and the names of places correctly.

(6) July 10 2001

Dear Terry,

   I am having fun on my trip. First we went to (7) Dallas Texas. Next we went to (8) Austin Texas. After that, my dad drove to (9) Santa Fe New Mexico. We saw an art museum and went to a concert there. I will be back soon!

      Your friend,
      Steve

Terry Jordan
326 North Verde Street
(10) Tempe Arizona 85280

Writing Connection

Neighborhood Sentences Draw a picture of a place that you have visited in your neighborhood. Write sentences about where you went, when you went, and what you did and saw. Remember to use commas (,) correctly.

Some programs add the date for you. Click on **Date and Time** under the **Insert** menu.

Extra Practice

Choose the correct verb to finish each sentence.

1. My parents let me (do, did) fun things.

2. We often (see, saw) plays.

3. Last month I (go, went) out with my parents.

4. We (see, saw) a great play then.

5. The actors we saw (do, did) a great job.

Rewrite the sentences. Put commas in the names of places and in the dates.

6. You can see many shows in New York New York.

7. I will see a show on November 22 2002.

8. Two actors in the show come from Los Angeles California.

9. Then I will go to Tampa Florida with my parents.

10. We will see a dance show on December 22 2002.

Language Play

Guess Where I Went!

● Think of two places you have visited and two places you want to visit. Make a chart like the one below.
● Take turns with a partner.
● Use the verbs *go, do,* and *see* to give hints about a place on your chart.
● Keep playing until both partners have guessed all the places.

Where I Went	Where I Want to Go
I went to the zoo. I went to Chicago, Illinois.	I want to go to New York, New York. I want to go to Mars.

Writing Connection

Write a Postcard Write a postcard about a town you like. Tell about what you do and see there and the places you go. Make sure you use verbs and commas (,) correctly.

July 22, 2001

Dear Anita,
I went to Santa Cruz, California. I left on July 10, 2001. I saw my grandpa and my grandma. We had fun!

Your friend,
Sara

Anita Ortega
245 West Street
New York, New York 10019

Chapter Review

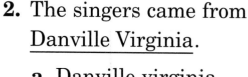

Choose the best answer for each underlined word or words.

1. Last week we <u>sees</u> singers at our school.

    a. saw

    b. saws

    c. see

    d. correct as is

2. The singers came from <u>Danville Virginia</u>.

    a. Danville virginia

    b. Danville, Virginia

    c. danville, Virginia

    d. correct as is

3. They <u>did</u> a great show.

    a. dids

    b. does

    c. done

    d. correct as is

4. It was on <u>May 11 2000</u>.

    a. May, 11 2000

    b. May 11, 2000

    c. May, 11, 2000

    d. correct as is

5. We <u>sees</u> them every year.

    a. saw

    b. sees

    c. see

    d. correct as is

6. The next show will be <u>May 9, 2001</u>.

    a. May, 9, 2001

    b. May, 9 2001

    c. May 9 2001

    d. correct as is

Visit our website for more activities with verbs:

www.harcourtschool.com

Study Skills

Using a Map

A **map** shows a place on paper. It can show a city, a state, or a country. A map is too small to show how things look. It uses little drawings instead. The **map key** tells what the drawings mean.

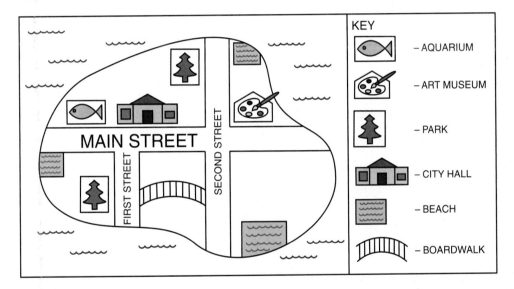

Practice

Use the map to answer the questions.

1. How many beaches are there?

2. How many parks are there?

3. Where can you find a boardwalk?

4. Where is the city hall?

5. How would you walk from the aquarium to the art museum?

Using Exact Words

Directions give steps to tell how to make or do something. The steps are written as commands.

Read these directions. Look at how the writer uses exact words to tell what to do.

from **Fire Fighters**
by Robert Maass

Fire fighters demonstrate how to *stop-drop-and-roll*. This is what you must do if your clothes catch on fire. **Stop:** Stop where you are. Don't run. **Drop:** Drop to the ground. **Roll:** Roll back and forth protecting your face with your hands to smother the flames.

Directions should be clear and easy to understand. **Exact words** tell readers what to do for each step. The steps should be easy for readers to picture in their minds.

Read these numbered directions.

In Case of Fire

1. Line up quietly.

2. Walk quickly to the nearest exit.

3. Go outside. Listen for instructions.

Think About It

1. How are both sets of directions alike? How are they different?

2. Could you picture the steps in your mind? Act out the first set of directions. Draw pictures for the second set of directions.

Using Exact Words

Exact words help readers follow directions correctly. When writers use exact words, readers can picture what to do at each step.

Roll: Roll back and forth protecting your face with your hands to smother the flames.

If the writer said only to roll, the reader would not know exactly what to do and why. This sentence tells the reader exactly how to roll.

A. Rewrite the directions below. Use exact words in place of the underlined word or words. Use the Word Bank for help.

1. This is how to make <u>something</u>.

2. Find <u>things</u>.

3. <u>Make</u> the paper in half.

4. Write <u>something on it</u>.

5. <u>Finish</u> the card.

Word Bank

- **bright-colored paper**
- **stickers**
- **a greeting on the front**
- **fold**
- **markers**
- **decorate**
- **a message inside**
- **a card**

B. Use exact words to complete these directions about how to mail a letter.

How to Mail a Letter

1. Put your letter in an envelope.

2. 1._____ the envelope.

3. Write the first and 2._____ name of the person to whom you are sending it.

4. Write the address 3._____ .

5. Put a stamp on the 4._____ corner of the envelope.

6. Drop the letter in a 5._____ .

)))) Writing and Thinking

Reflect Tell what helped you think of exact words. Did you picture the steps in your mind before you wrote? Write your ideas. Share your ideas in a small group.

Applying the Craft

TAAS SKILL

Read these directions. Think about how the exact words that are underlined help the reader know just what to do.

What to Do When the Morning Bell Rings

1. Line up by the <u>front door</u>. Stand in <u>ABC order by last name</u>.

2. <u>March single file</u> into the classroom.

3. Sit in your <u>assigned seat</u>.

Looking at the Model

1. Which parts of these directions give the reader the best idea of what to do? Why?

2. What could happen if the writer had not used exact words? Why?

Your Turn

Write directions for a new student about how to do something in your school.

Prewriting and Drafting

STEP 1 **Develop your ideas.**

Ask yourself these questions.

• What must be done first, next, and last?

• What are the best words to tell how to do each step?

STEP 2 **Brainstorm exact words.**

Make a flowchart. Add exact words to show your reader what to do.

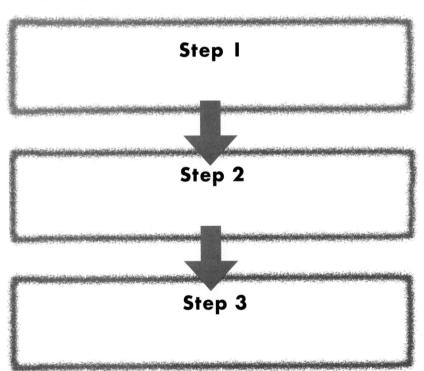

Step 1

Step 2

Step 3

What Good Writers Do

☑ Remember to tell your readers exactly what to do.

☑ Put your ideas in the correct order.

Student Handbook

Use the thesaurus on page 494 to help you think of exact words.

STEP 3 **Write your draft.**

Use your chart and What Good Writers Do to write a draft of your directions.

Editing Your Directions

Share your draft with a few classmates. Together, talk about how you can make your directions better. Use the checklist and the Editor's Marks to help you revise your directions.

☑ My directions are in the correct order.

☑ My directions use exact words so that my reader knows what to do.

Editor's Marks

∧ Add.

⅄ Change.

℘ Take out.

= Use a capital letter.

⊙ Add a period.

◯ Check the spelling.

Sharing with Others

Meet with a partner or in a small group. Read your directions aloud. Have others follow the directions.

•Handwriting•

Retracing Letters Correctly

Follow these tips to make sure your letters with retraced strokes are formed correctly.

correct	incorrect
Building	Building

✓ Try not to lift your pencil from the paper.

✓ Retrace along the same line.

✓ Do not put any loops in these letters or leave any spaces.

✓ Make the strokes smooth and even.

Write these letters and words. Use your best handwriting. Follow the tips to make the strokes correctly.

B h m n r u

Build a tree house.

Bake the muffins.

What Is a Helping Verb?

Read this short play.

Who Has Made the Painting?

Characters:	brush, paint, pencil
Time:	evening
Setting:	in the artist's toolbox

Brush: I have painted the mural on the wall.

Paint: Not true! I have painted it. I have covered the wall with beautiful colors.

Pencil: I had started it. I had traced the lines of the drawings.

Paint: I have filled those lines with color. The brush has helped me, but it did not paint.

Brush: How would you get on the wall without me? You need me.

Pencil: Let's not argue! I think we forgot a few things.

Brush and Paint: What?

Pencil: The artist has guided me on the wall. She has picked the paint, and she has brushed it on. The *artist* has created the painting!

Read the play aloud with two partners. Act out each action.

> A **helping verb** works with the main verb to tell about an action.
>
> The artist **has** <u>painted</u> the flower red.
>
> *Has* is the helping verb.

Write a helping verb and a main verb to complete each new line of the play.

Brush: First the artist _____ the paint.

Paint: Next she _____ the lines with the pencil.

Pencil: Then she _____ the brush into the paint.

Think about what might happen next. Work with your partners to add new lines to the play. Include helping verbs.

Using *Has*, *Have*, and *Had*

Use the helping verbs **has**, **have**, and **had** with other verbs to show action that happened in the past.

- **Has** tells about one.

    Tim **has helped** our teacher.

- **Have** tells about more than one and is used with *I*.

    All the children **have worked** hard.
    I **have worked** hard, too.

- **Had** tells about one or more than one.

    Tanya **had cleaned** her desk before.
    Don and Felipe **had helped** yesterday.

Guided Practice

Choose the correct helping verb to finish each sentence.

1. The children (have, has) cleaned the classroom.

2. The teacher (had, have) asked them to do so.

3. David (has, have) picked up the trash.

4. Victor and Yoko (had, has) wiped the board.

5. The children (have, has) washed everything.

Independent Practice

Choose the correct helping verb to finish each sentence.

6. The parents (have, has) walked into our classroom.

7. Our teacher (has, have) talked to the parents.

8. Pablo (had, have) asked to sing a song.

9. My dad (had, have) wished to see my work.

10. He (has, have) stopped by my desk with my mom.

11. First my parents (has, have) listened to Pablo's song.

12. Then they (has, have) looked at my papers.

Writing Connection

Writing a Summary Think about a story you like. Write a few sentences to tell the main events that happened. Use the helping verbs *has*, *have*, and *had*.

The Lost Island

Write your summary on your computer. Save it and label the disk to help you find the document later.

Keeping to One Main Idea

A paragraph is a group of sentences that tell about one **main idea**. The first sentence of a paragraph often gives the main idea. The other sentences give **details**. They tell more about the main idea.

Painting a picture takes time. First think about what you want to paint. Next make a few drawings in pencil. Pick the best drawing, and draw it again on good paper. Then mix your colors and paint your picture.

Guided Practice

Write the paragraph. Underline the main idea. Leave out the sentence that does not tell about the main idea.

1.   Paintings can be found in many different places. You can see them at a museum or an art gallery. You can also go to an art show in a park or at school. Red roses are beautiful flowers. Paintings are in books, too.

Independent Practice

Write each paragraph. Underline the main idea. Leave out the sentence that does not tell about the main idea.

2. I have made a penguin puppet. First I picked some black and white felt. I like ducks, too. I used the felt to make the body. Then I added a piece of orange paper for the beak and two little paper eyes. Last I glued some black felt on each side to make the wings.

3. I worked hard to get ready for my part in the play. Before the show, I had learned my lines. I also had practiced many times with my partners. I had learned how to move on stage. My friend made a penguin puppet. By the day of the play, I was ready to go.

Writing Connection

Revising Choose a paragraph from your Writing Portfolio. Make sure all the sentences tell about one main idea. Cross out any sentences that do not tell about the main idea.

Press `tab` once to indent a paragraph on your computer.

Extra Practice

Copy each sentence. Underline the helping verb. Then circle the verb it helps.

1. We have decided to recycle.

2. Our teacher had talked to us about it.

3. We have placed three trash cans in the classroom.

Choose the correct helping verb to finish each sentence.

4. The children (have, has) reused old things.

5. Tim and Laura (have, has) cleaned old cans.

6. They (has, have) used them to hold pencils.

7. Kim (had, have) wanted a box for stickers.

8. She (had, has) made a box from egg cartons.

9. The children (has, have) helped their school.

Write the paragraph. Underline the main idea. Leave out the sentence that does not tell about the main idea.

10. My brother and I had worked in the park last Saturday. We put out seeds for the birds. My mom reads often. We weeded the flower garden.

Language Play

Helping Verbs Calendar

- Write *have*, *has*, and *had* on three strips of paper. Place them in a bag.
- Find or draw a calendar showing the past week.
- Take turns with a partner. Pick a helping verb. Use it in a sentence. Tell about one helpful thing you did last week.
- Keep playing until you have each said a sentence for each day of the week.

Sunday	Monday	Tuesday	Wednesday	Thursday	Friday	Saturday

Writing Connection

Functional Writing: Job Chart Make a list of jobs for you and your classmates. Share it with the group. Decide who does each job. Then hang up the job chart.

Job Chart

wipe board	Joe
water the plants	Tara
pick up trash	Susana
clean hamster cage	Chris

Chapter Review

Choose the best answer for the underlined words.

1. Last month, the mayor
<u>had walked</u> in the park.

   a. have walked

   b. hads walked

   c. haves walked

   d. correct as is

2. She saw that children
<u>has used</u> a dirty park.

   a. had used

   b. haves used

   c. have used

   d. correct as is

3. She <u>have planned</u> a
"Park Clean-Up Day."

   a. haves planned

   b. has planned

   c. hads planned

   d. correct as is

4. My friends <u>has cleaned</u>
the playground last year.

   a. had cleaned

   b. haves cleaned

   c. have has cleaned

   d. correct as is

5. This year we <u>have started</u>
to work in the park.

   a. haves started

   b. hads started

   c. has started

   d. correct as is

6. The mayor <u>have agreed</u>
to help.

   a. has agreed

   b. haves agreed

   c. hads agreed

   d. correct as is

 **Visit our website for more
activities with helping verbs:**
www.harcourtschool.com

▣ Technology ▣

Using Computer Graphics

You can use your computer to add graphics, or pieces of art, to your writing.

- **Use different kinds of type.** Using different kinds of type and different colors makes writing fun to read.

- **Add pictures to a story.** Use pictures from your word processing program, or use a separate drawing program. Add art to your story to make a book.

- **Add frames and borders.**

- **Add charts or graphs to a report.** Use your computer to make charts and graphs. Show them as you share your report with your classmates.

Practice

1. Pick a piece of writing from your Writing Portfolio.

2. Add graphics and publish your writing.

What Is an Adverb?

Read the dialogue.

Who's Been Sleeping in My Porridge?

"Who's been sitting in my bed?"
      said the mama bear crossly.
"Who's been eating my chair?"
      said the baby bear weepily.
"Who's been sleeping in my porridge?"
      said the papa bear angrily.
"Wait a minute," said Goldilocks.

"Why can't you guys just stick
      to the script? Now let's try it
      again and this time, no messing around."

Colin McNaughton

Words like *angrily* and *happily* can help describe how someone does something. Think about times you have felt sad, happy, or excited. Show or tell about the different ways you can say something. Then list words that tell the ways you felt.

> An **adverb** describes a verb. It can tell *how, when,* or *where* an action takes place.
>
> I sang **joyfully**.
> I **quietly** whispered.

Add a new part to the dialogue. Write what the character says. Write an adverb to tell how the character says it. Then act out your new lines with a partner.

"Who's been _____?"

said the mama bear _____.

"Who's been _____?"

said the baby bear _____.

"Who's been _____?"

said the papa bear _____.

Using Adverbs

Use an adverb to tell *how*, *when*, or *where* an action takes place.

The child played **quietly**. *how*
She played **inside**. *where*
Her aunt visited **today**. *when*

Here are some more adverbs.

How?	When?	Where?
loudly	always	far
carefully	sometimes	near
proudly	often	inside
softly	soon	outside

Guided Practice

Look at the adverb in each sentence. Write *how*, *when*, or *where* for each adverb.

1. We want to put on a play <u>soon</u>.

2. We have to practice <u>often</u>.

3. We all say our lines <u>loudly</u>.

4. Our teacher <u>carefully</u> chooses the actors.

5. We will try on our costumes <u>inside</u>.

Independent Practice

Look at the adverb in each sentence. Write *how*, *when*, or *where* for each adverb.

6. Carmen waited <u>near</u> the stage.

7. She <u>slowly</u> walked up to the stage.

8. Carmen said her lines <u>proudly</u>.

9. Jenny draws <u>beautifully</u>.

10. Ms. Brown chose her <u>yesterday</u> to draw scenery.

11. <u>Today</u> we start practicing.

12. We practiced <u>inside</u> our classroom.

13. The first practice went <u>badly</u>.

14. <u>Sometimes</u> we forgot our lines.

15. We learned our lines <u>quickly</u>.

Writing Connection

Lively Adverbs Draw a picture or choose one from an old magazine. Write sentences to tell what is happening. Use a lively adverb in each sentence to describe the action.

Use your computer to help you add adverbs to your sentences.

Writing with Adverbs

> Adverbs always give more details. When you tell *how, when,* or *where,* you give more information to the reader.

Guided Practice

Add an adverb that answers the question in ( ). Write the new sentence.

1. Debbie reads her lines. (How?)

2. Mr. Reed checks the lights. (When?)

3. Tammy puts on make-up. (How?)

4. Joey ties the sash on his costume. (How?)

5. Ms. Brown plays her piano. (Where?)

Independent Practice

Add an adverb that answers the question in ( ). Write the new sentence.

6. Josh wrote the program. (When?)

7. Ms. Brown made copies of the program. (How?)

8. Sam passed out the programs. (When?)

9. The teacher moved the scenery. (Where?)

10. The actors were waiting. (Where?)

11. People came to the theater. (When?)

12. They gave their tickets to Sam. (How?)

13. The people sat. (How?)

14. The lights went out. (How?)

15. The curtain went up. (When?)

Writing Connection

Revising Look through your Writing Portfolio to find a piece of writing you like. Where can you add more details that tell *how, where,* and *when*? Revise your writing. Use adverbs.

Use your computer to write. Then it's easy to make changes until you are happy with your writing.

Extra Practice

Underline the adverb in each sentence.

1. The principal warmly welcomed the people.

2. The music started softly.

3. Each actor spoke loudly.

4. Children moved the scenery quietly.

Look at the adverb in each sentence. Write *how*, *when*, or *where* for each adverb.

5. The people laughed <u>happily</u> at the funny parts.

6. They listened <u>quietly</u> at the sad parts.

7. Sam helped with costumes <u>behind</u> the curtain.

8. <u>Soon</u> Ms. Brown played the music.

Add an adverb to each sentence to give more details.

9. The children were smiling.

10. Everyone was clapping.

Language Play

Adverb Challenge

- Take turns with a partner. Roll a number cube.
- Choose an adverb from the correct column. Use it in a sentence. You get one point if you use the adverb correctly.
- The first player with 5 points wins.

1 or 4	2 or 5	3 or 6
How?	When?	Where?
slowly	early	here
fast	soon	inside
warmly	then	below
loudly	now	far
clearly	next	down

Writing Connection

News Story A news story tells about something that really happened. It answers the questions *who, what, when, where, why,* and *how.* Write a short news story about something you saw. Use adverbs. Use this news story as a model.

Heavy Rain Falls in River City

Yesterday the rain began suddenly. People ran quickly to find shelter. The storm moved through fast. Soon the sun shone brightly in the sky again.

Chapter Review

STANDARDIZED TEST PREP

Choose the best answer to finish each sentence.

1. Ms. Brown praised the class _____.

   a. warm

   b. warmly

   c. under

2. The children had worked _____.

   a. hard

   b. difficult

   c. ever

3. They want to start another play _____.

   a. coldly

   b. above

   c. soon

4. They finish their schoolwork _____.

   a. far

   b. quickly

   c. around

5. The children are _____ reading plays.

   a. eagerly

   b. near

   c. last

6. They hope to choose a new play _____.

   a. tomorrow

   b. near

   c. last

Visit our website for more activities with adverbs:

www.harcourtschool.com

∎Study Skills∎

Using the Library

The library puts books in a special order. It also puts fiction books and nonfiction books in separate places.

- **Fiction books** are made-up stories. They are in ABC order by the author's last name.
- **Nonfiction books** are about things that are real. They are put in order by topic and then by their special numbers.

 You can use a computer to help you find books in a library.

Practice

In which part of the library would you find each book? Write *fiction* or *nonfiction*.

fiction

nonfiction

1. 582 *Endangered Plants* by Jeff Sanders
2. *Digger Dog* by Tom McNeal
3. 419 *The Handtalk School* by Mary Beth Miller
4. *Swimmy* by Leo Lionni

Look at the books in items 1-4.

5. Write the fiction book titles in ABC order.
6. Write the nonfiction book titles in order.

Notable
Social Studies
Book

How can you tell someone how to do something? One way is to explain the steps. Pablo helps to make different kinds of bread in this story. Find out the steps he follows.

from Jalapeño Bagels

by Natasha Wing   illustrated by Robert Casilla

"What should I bring to school on Monday for International Day?" I ask my mother. "My teacher told us to bring something from our culture."

"You can bring a treat from the *panaderia*," she suggests. Panaderia is what Mama calls our bakery. "Help us bake on Sunday—then you can pick out whatever you want."

"It's a deal," I tell her. I like helping at the bakery. It's warm there, and everything smells so good.

Early Sunday morning, when it is still dark, my mother wakes me up.

"Pablo, it's time to go to work," she says.

We walk down the street to the bakery. My father turns on the lights. My mother turns on the ovens. She gets out the pans and ingredients for *pan dulce*. Pan dulce is Mexican sweet bread.

I help my mother mix and knead the dough. She shapes rolls and loaves of bread and slides them into the oven. People tell her she makes the best pan dulce in town.

"Maybe I'll bring pan dulce to school," I tell her.

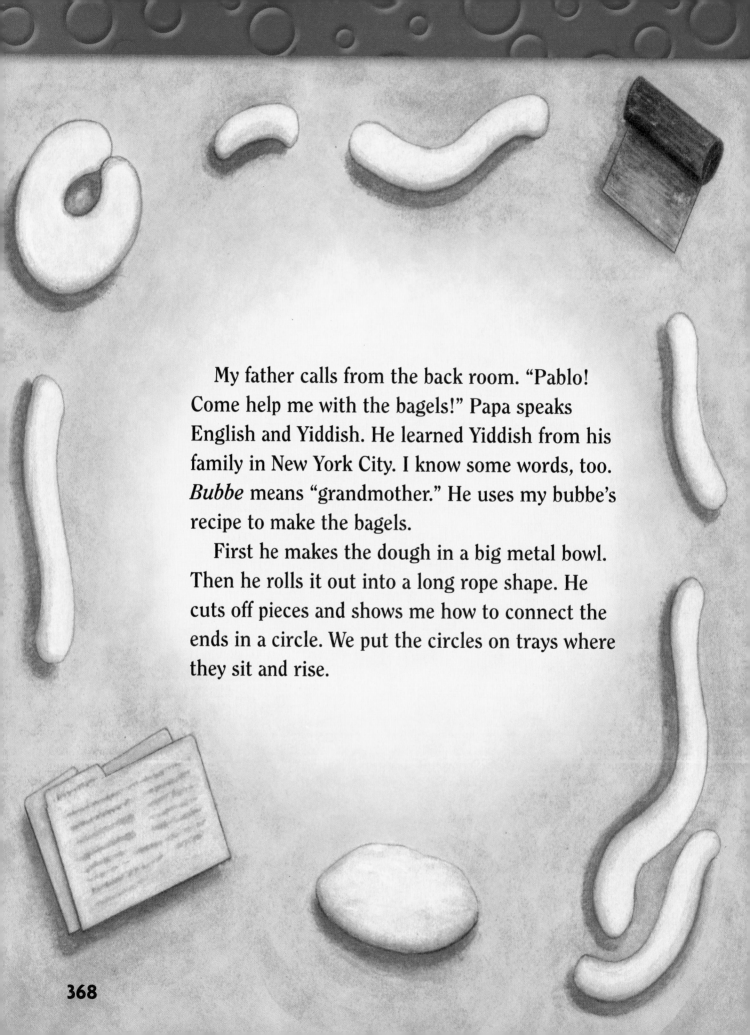

My father calls from the back room. "Pablo! Come help me with the bagels!" Papa speaks English and Yiddish. He learned Yiddish from his family in New York City. I know some words, too. *Bubbe* means "grandmother." He uses my bubbe's recipe to make the bagels.

First he makes the dough in a big metal bowl. Then he rolls it out into a long rope shape. He cuts off pieces and shows me how to connect the ends in a circle. We put the circles on trays where they sit and rise.

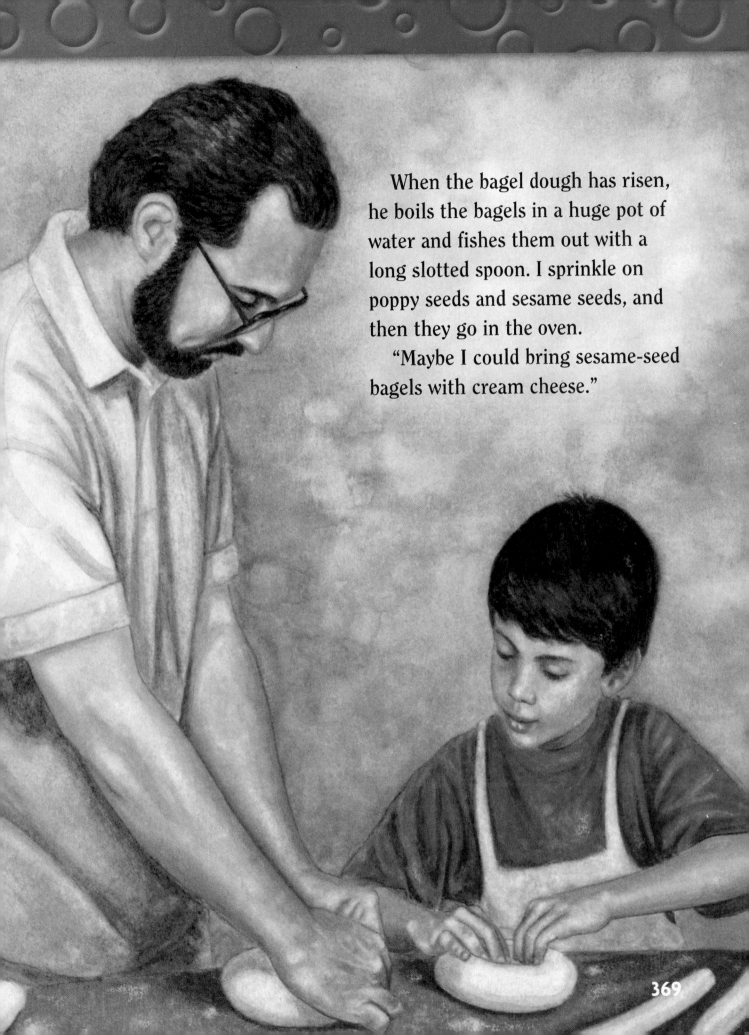

When the bagel dough has risen, he boils the bagels in a huge pot of water and fishes them out with a long slotted spoon. I sprinkle on poppy seeds and sesame seeds, and then they go in the oven.

"Maybe I could bring sesame-seed bagels with cream cheese."

369

My mother joins us and helps my father make another batch of bagels—*jalapeño* bagels. My parents use their own special recipe. While Papa kneads the dough, Mama chops the jalapeño *chiles*. She tosses them into the dough and adds dried red peppers. We roll, cut, make circles, and let them rise. I can't wait until they are done because I am getting hungry.

"Have you decided what you're going to bring to school?" asks Mama.

"It's hard to choose. Everything is so good," I tell her.

"You should decide before we open," warns Mama, "or else our customers will buy everything up."

I walk past all the sweet breads and bagels.

I think about my mother and my father and all the different things they make in the bakery.

Suddenly I know exactly what I'm going to bring.

"Jalapeño bagels," I tell my parents. "I'll spread them with cream cheese and jam."

"Why jalapeño bagels?" asks Papa.

"Because they are a mixture of both of you. Just like me!"

Think About It

1. What do you think of Pablo's choice for what to bring for International Day?

2. What was the most surprising thing you learned about making bagels?

Parts of a How-to Paragraph

In a **how-to paragraph**, a writer gives steps to tell how to make or do something.

- The first sentence tells what the paragraph will explain how to do.
- The second sentence tells all the things you need.
- The **steps** are written in the order they should be done. Time-order words make their order clear.

Reread this how-to paragraph from the story. Then, on a sheet of paper, complete the flowchart.

First he makes the dough in a big metal bowl. Then he rolls it out into a long rope shape. He cuts off pieces and shows me how to connect the ends in a circle. We put the circles on trays where they sit and rise.

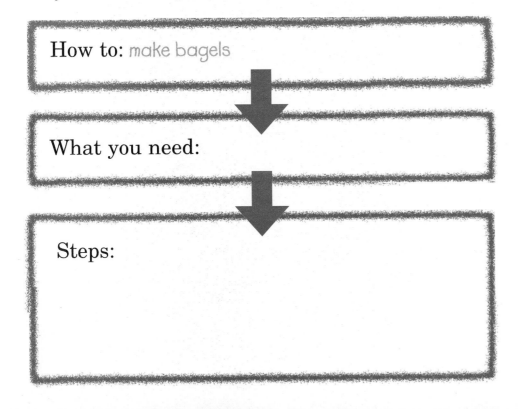

How to: make bagels

What you need:

Steps:

A Student Model

TAAS SKILL

Maria enjoyed learning how to make bagels. She thought of something she could teach her classmates to make. Read her how-to paragraph, and see how she put the important parts in order.

How to Make Fun Dough

You can make your own fun dough. You need two cups of salt, two cups of warm water, two cups of flour, a bowl, and food coloring. First put the water in the bowl and add a little food coloring. Next put the salt and flour slowly into the bowl. Then mix the dough with your hands. Play with the dough, or put it in the refrigerator to keep it fresh.

The **title** tells what the paragraph will help the reader make.

The **materials** are what you need to do the activity.

The **steps** tell what to do in the correct order.

Looking at the Model

1. What is Maria's paragraph about?

2. What do you need to make fun dough?

3. What is the first step?

4. What is the second step?

5. What do you do after everything is in the bowl?

Writer's Craft

Using Exact Words

Maria made sure her how-to paragraph was easy to understand. She used exact words to show how and when to do all the steps. Find the parts of Maria's paragraph that have exact words.

- How much salt and flour do you need? How do you know?

- How do you know when to add flour and salt?

- When do you mix everything together? What do you use to mix the dough?

Writing Workshop

Prewriting

Before Maria wrote her how-to paragraph, she planned it. She knew it was important to list all the materials and steps. She used a flowchart to plan her paragraph and put her ideas in order.

How to: make fun dough

⬇

What you need: two cups of salt, two cups of warm water, two cups of flour, a bowl, food coloring

⬇

Steps: First put the water in the bowl. Add food coloring.

Next put the salt and flour into the bowl.

Then mix the dough with your hands.

Last play with the dough, or put it in the refrigerator to keep it fresh.

Yur Turn

STEP 1 **Think of things you can make or do.** Make a list of snacks or crafts you like to make. Write or draw your ideas.

STEP 2 **Choose one thing about which to write.** Choose something your classmates would like to learn to do.

STEP 3 **Complete a flowchart.**

What Good Writers Do

 Remember for whom you are writing and why.

✓ Make a plan that shows the steps in the order in which you will write them.

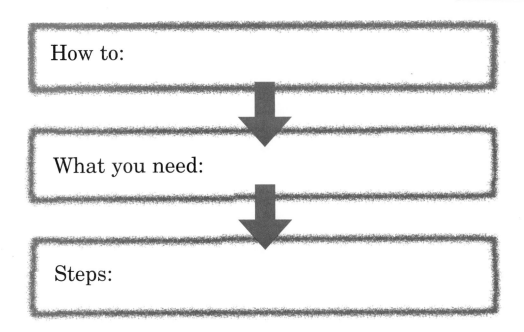

How to:

↓

What you need:

↓

Steps:

Drafting

Maria used her flowchart to help her write a first draft. She wrote her ideas quickly. Later she could go back over her work and correct any mistakes.

DRAFT

How to Make Fun Dough

You can make your own fun dough. You need two cups of salt, two cups of warm water, two cups of flour, a bowl, and food coloring. First put the water in the bowl and add a little food coloring. And then put the salt and flour slowly into the bowl. Play with the dough. Mix the dough with your hands.

Look at the way Maria's how-to paragraph follows her flowchart so far. What else can she add to make it complete?

How to: make fun dough

↓

What you need: two cups of salt, two cups of warm water, two cups of flour, a bowl, food coloring

↓

Steps: First put the water in the bowl. Add food coloring.

Next put the salt and flour into the bowl.

Then mix the dough with your hands.

Last play with the dough, or put it in the refrigerator to keep it fresh.

Your Turn

Use your flowchart and What Good Writers Do to write a draft of a how-to paragraph.

Remember to put the date on your draft. It will help you tell which draft is newer.

Revising

Maria read her draft to a partner. Her partner gave her some ideas about how to make her writing better. Look at how Maria revised her how-to paragraph.

What Good Writers Do

 Check that the paragraph has a topic sentence and a list of the things you need.

 Make sure the steps are in order.

 Make sure that you used time-order words.

(DRAFT) **How to Make Fun Dough**

You can make your own fun dough. You need two cups of salt, two cups of warm water, two cups of flour, a bowl, and food coloring. First put the water in the bowl and add a little food
Next
coloring. And then put the salt and flour slowly
Then
into the bowl. ⟨Play with the dough.⟩ Mix the dough with your hands. Or put it in the refrigerator to keeep it fresh.

Editor's Marks

∧   **Add.**

⋀   **Change.**

⌐   **Take out.**

⬭   **Move.**

Your Turn

Read your own how-to paragraph again. Use What Good Writers Do and the Editor's Marks to fix any mistakes.

Proofreading

Maria read her how-to paragraph one more time to look for other mistakes. Think about why she made each change in red.

DRAFT **How to Make Fun Dough**

You can make your own fun dough. You need two cups of salt, two cups of warm water, two cups of flour, a bowl, and food coloring. First put the water in the bowl and add a little food coloring. ~~And then~~ Next put the salt and flour slowly into the bowl. Play with the dough. Then Mix the dough with your hands. Or put it in the refrigerator to keep ~~keeep~~ it fresh.

What Good Writers Do

 Remember to leave margins to make the writing easy to read.

 Check that you used adverbs to help tell how to do a step.

 Check to see if you left out capital letters or need to make a letter lowercase.

 Check spelling.

Editor's Marks

 Add a comma.

 Use a capital letter.

/ Make a lowercase letter.

 Check the spelling.

Your Turn

Read your own how-to paragraph again. Use What Good Writers Do and the Editor's Marks to fix any mistakes.

Revise and edit your draft on the computer.

Publishing

Maria decided to make a poster to show other children how to make fun dough. First she copied her how-to paragraph onto large paper. Then she added a colorful title. Last she drew a picture to show each step.

Y☺ur Turn

Make a clean copy of your how-to paragraph. Make all the changes. Use a computer if you want. Here are some more ideas for publishing your how-to paragraph.

- **Make a class book.**
  Put your final copy with your classmates' work into a booklet. Work together to make a cover with art and a title. Place the booklet in a how-to corner of the classroom library.

- **Send an e-mail.**
  Copy your how-to paragraph into an e-mail to a friend who likes to make things. Ask your teacher or a family member if you may send the e-mail.

Put your finished how-to paragraph in your Writing Portfolio.

Listening and Speaking

Giving and Following Directions

You can present your how-to paragraph to a group. Practice these tips.

Tips for Giving Directions

- Think about the steps and their order before you begin speaking.
- Start by telling the main idea.
- Tell about what is needed. Show each object, if you can.
- Tell the steps in order. Use time-order words such as *first*, *next*, *then*, and *last*.
- Use objects, pictures, and hand motions to show what to do for each step.
- Answer any questions about the directions.

Tips for Following Directions

- Listen carefully to all the steps.
- Try to picture each step as you hear it.
- Listen for time-order words such as *first*, *next*, *then*, and *last*.
- Ask questions if you do not understand.
- Follow the steps.

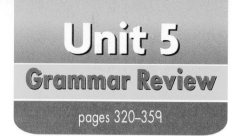

Using *Come*, *Run*, and *Give* pages 320–321

Write the correct verb in ( ) to complete each sentence.

1. Dad (comes, came) home from his trip now.

2. When we see him, Amy and I (run, ran) outside to greet him.

3. Last month he (gives, gave) us gifts from a museum store.

Joining Sentences pages 322–323

Use *and* to join the sentences. Remember to use a comma (,) before *and*.

4. A taxi pulled up. Amy saw that it was Dad.

5. Dad came home early. We gave him a hug.

Using *Go*, *Do*, and *See* pages 330–331

Write the correct verb in ( ) to complete each sentence.

6. Last year Dad (go, went) to the theater often.

7. He (see, saw) many famous actors.

8. Now Dad (does, did) some work for our school plays.

Commas in Place Names and Dates pages 332–333

Write the dates and the names of places correctly.

9. Today is May 28 2001.

10. Mom is at an art show in Provo Utah.

Using *Has*, *Have*, and *Had* pages 348–349

Choose the correct helping verb in ( ) to complete each sentence.

11. Mina (has, have) acted in a play.

12. We (has, have) watched her new show.

13. Last week I (had, has) painted a sign for the show.

Keeping to One Main Idea pages 350–351

Rewrite the paragraph. Underline the main idea. Leave out the sentence that does not tell about the main idea.

14. Last week I went to the Children's Museum. I saw many old toys. I also looked at some children's drawings. My sister gave me a book last month. I had a good time at the museum.

Using Adverbs pages 358–359

Read the adverb in each sentence. Then write *how*, *when*, or *where* for each adverb.

15. Time passes <u>quickly</u> at the museum.

16. I have fun <u>here</u>.

17. We will return <u>soon</u>.

Writing with Adverbs pages 360–361

Add an adverb that answers the question in ( ).

18. We line up to leave the museum. (When?)

19. Carla and Tim put on their coats. (Where?)

Math

Let's Go on a Trip!

Does your class want to go on a field trip to an art museum, a concert, or a show? Do you need to raise money to pay for the trip? Here are some ideas for how you might do this.

Plan the Trip

- Where do you want to go? Why do you want to go there? Get information from the museum, theater, or place you want to visit.

- Find out how much money you will need to raise. How much will the bus ride cost? How much are the tickets?

Plan the Fund-Raiser

- Decide what kind of fund-raiser you want to have. Will it be a bake sale, a fun run, or some other event?

- Make a plan. List the steps you need to take to hold the event.

- Talk to your principal about your field trip and your fund-raiser. Tell him or her why your class wants to go on the trip and why you need to raise money. Explain your plan.

Follow Your Plan

- Talk with parents and other people who can help. Explain what they can do.

- Get the word out about your fund-raiser. Make posters and send e-mails that will get people to come to your event.

- Hold your event. Then have a great time on your trip!

Books to Read

If You Made a Million
by David M. Schwartz
Nonfiction
This book tells about the many ways money is used.
ALA Notable Book, Teachers' Choice

A Money Adventure: Earning, Saving, Spending, Sharing
by Neale S. Godfrey
Nonfiction
A group of children finds out how money is earned, saved, spent, and shared.

Unit 6

Grammar
- Usage Wrap-Up

Writing
- Book Report
- Research Report

All About Dinosaurs

The word *dinosaur* means "terrible lizard." The first dinosaurs lived more than 200 million years ago. The dinosaurs died out about 65 million years ago, though. Scientists learn about dinosaurs from fossils they find in the ground.

See

• Dinosaur Family Tree

• The Biggest and Smallest Dinosaurs

• What Happened to the Dinosaurs?

gosaurus

saurus had a narrow body and a heavy, spiked tail.
ack legs were almost twice as long as its front legs.
planteater may have reared on its hind legs to reach
vegetation.

saurus armatus

Nouns and Pronouns Together

Read the poem.

The Mockingbird

The mockingbird, the mockingbird,
In the morning he speaks, in the morning
    he sings.
For the sake of the people in the morning
    he speaks,
In the morning he sings.

from the Acoma nation

Read the poem with a partner. Talk about what the bird in the poem does. Then tell about other things birds do at different times of the day.

A **pronoun** is a word that takes the place of a noun. *I*, *he*, *she*, *they*, and *it* are pronouns. Each pronoun in a sentence should go with the noun it replaces.

Teresa watches a **mockingbird**. **She** draws a picture of **it**.

Think about a person you like. Write this person's name twice on the first line. Then add new lines to the poem. Use some pronouns to tell what the person does.

————————, ————————,

In the morning ——————————, in the morning

——————————.

For the sake of the people in the morning

——————————,

In the morning ——————————.

Noun-Pronoun Agreement

A pronoun is a word that takes the place of a noun. A pronoun should agree with, or go with, the noun it replaces.

Ms. Gomez is a scientist.
She studies rocks.

The rocks are rough.
They are hard to climb.

Guided Practice

Write the pronoun that agrees with the underlined noun in each set of sentences.

1. The <u>families</u> went camping.
   _____ had a good time.

2. <u>Maria</u> took her sleeping bag.
   _____ knew it would keep her warm.

3. <u>José</u> brought a telescope.
   _____ wanted to see stars.

4. The <u>telescope</u> was small and black.
   _____ helped José see stars and planets.

 A pronoun should agree with the noun it replaces.

Independent Practice

Write the pronoun that agrees with the underlined noun in each set of sentences.

5. The <u>grown-ups</u> set up the tents.
_____ worked hard.

6. The <u>tents</u> were large.
_____ were big enough for four people.

7. <u>Barbara</u> went to collect wood.
_____ came back with many dry sticks.

8. <u>Mr. Johnson</u> built a fire in the fire pit.
Then _____ lit the fire with a match.

9. The <u>wood</u> crackled as it burned.
_____ made a warm fire.

10. <u>Mrs. Johnson</u> unpacked the food.
Then _____ helped make dinner.

Writing Connection

Revising Choose a piece of writing from your Writing Portfolio. Find nouns that you can replace with pronouns. Make sure your pronouns agree.

 You can use your computer to edit. Erase a letter or word by pressing the `delete` key.

393

Word Order for Pronouns

When you talk or write about another person and yourself using **I** or **me**, always name yourself last. Use **I** in the naming part of the sentence.

> **Bob and I** went to the store.

Use **me** in the telling part.

> Mr. Flores gave apples to **Bob and me**.

Guided Practice

Write the correct words in ( ) to complete each sentence.

1. (My family and I, I and my family) flew to the Grand Canyon.

2. My sister Lisa sat next to (my mother and me, me and my mother) on the jet.

3. (I and Lisa, Lisa and I) had never been to the Grand Canyon.

4. My mother read a book about it to (me and Lisa, Lisa and me).

Independent Practice

Write the correct words in ( ) to complete each sentence.

5. (My family and I, I and my family) hiked to the bottom of the canyon.

6. My mother let (Lisa and me, me and Lisa) carry our own water.

7. (I and my father, My father and I) saw a mule.

8. My mother asked (my sister and me, me and my sister) if we wanted to ride it.

9. (Lisa and I, I and Lisa) took turns riding.

10. (My family and I, I and my family) had a great trip.

Writing Connection

Using Clear Pronouns Write sentences about a trip you took. Tell about things you did and with whom you did them. Make sure the pronouns and nouns you use together are in the correct order.

Use your computer to help you write. Save your writing, and add more details later.

Extra Practice

Write the pronoun that agrees with the underlined noun in each set of sentences.

1. The <u>children</u> went hiking with their parents.

   _____ carried backpacks.

2. <u>Cindy</u> had the map.

   _____ led the way.

3. First the <u>path</u> went by two lakes.

   Next _____ passed through the woods.

4. An <u>eagle</u> flew in the sky.

   Then _____ landed in a tall tree.

5. <u>Tom and Kim</u> were last.

   _____ had to run to catch up.

Write the correct words in ( ) to complete each sentence.

6. (Luis and I, I and Luis) saw a deer.

7. The deer walked close to (Luis and me, me and Luis).

8. (Wu and I, I and Wu) listened to the birds.

9. The birds sang to (me and Wu, Wu and me).

10. (Pat and I, I and Pat) watched the chipmunks.

Pronoun Partners

- Write sentences on cards.
- Pick a card. Read the sentence to a partner.
- Your partner changes one noun in the sentence to a pronoun and says the new sentence.
- Then switch places with your partner.
- You get one point for each correct sentence.

Many ducks swim in the lake.

Diane and Paul are going to the lake.

Liz likes to watch birds.

The boy and his family went to the park.

Writing Connection

Play Dialogue Work with a classmate. Talk to each other about something that you and other classmates did together. Use pronouns when you talk. Write what you say in play form.

Teresa:	Han and I went to the park yesterday.
Stella:	Beth and I did, too. She and I fed the ducks.
Teresa:	Han and I saw the ducks, too! He told me
	about the different kinds of ducks.

Chapter Review

Choose the best answer for the underlined word or words.

1. Matt went to camp. <u>He</u> had never been there before.

   a. She

   b. It

   c. correct as is

2. Matt and Donny wanted to go to the lake. <u>It</u> hoped to catch fish.

   a. She

   b. They

   c. correct as is

3. The children sat around a campfire. <u>She</u> listened to stories.

   a. It

   b. They

   c. correct as is

4. The campers did a skit. <u>They</u> played the parts of a rabbit and a bear.

   a. It

   b. He

   c. correct as is

5. <u>I and Matt</u> took a hike with Ms. Jones.

   a. Matt and I

   b. Matt

   c. correct as is

6. She showed <u>me and Matt</u> new trails.

   a. Me

   b. Matt and me

   c. correct as is

Visit our website for more activities
with using nouns and pronouns:
www.harcourtschool.com

▣ Study Skills ▣

Using a Telephone Book

A **telephone book** has the phone numbers and addresses of people and businesses. Use the guide words at the top of the page to find the page you need. The people's last names are in alphabetical order.

Hale—Hapford	
HALE Nathan 1 Elm St 555-0198	**HALFORD Sally** 22 West St 555-0164
HALE Robert 24 Main St 555-0110	**HALGAN Chris** 774 Oak St 555-0151
HALEY Bill 36 South St . . . 555-0156	**HALLER G.** 7 South St 555-0192
HALFON Tom 4 North St 555-0103	**HAO David** 43 Main St 555-0122

Practice

Use the telephone book page above to answer each question.

1. What is Nathan Hale's telephone number?

2. Who lives at 774 Oak Street?

3. Who else could be on this page — Stephen Glenn, Carol Hall, or Howard Jackson?

4. Where would Kim Hammond go on this page?

Subject-Verb Agreement

Read the poem.

Sun Song

Birds in the branches hear the sun's first song.
Ranitas in the rocks hear the sun's first song.
Bees in the bushes hear the sun's first song.
Wind in the willows hears the sun's first song.

Birds in the branches chirp their morning song.
Ranitas in the rocks croak their morning song.
Bees in the bushes buzz their morning song.
Wind in the willows whirrs its morning song.

Sun song. Sun song. Sun song.

Pat Mora

Work with a group. Make up a tune and sing "Sun Song" or act out your favorite part. Then say more sentences to go with the poem.

A verb should always **agree** with, or go with, the naming part of a sentence. When the naming part of a sentence tells about one, add **s** to the verb.

The cat **meows** its morning song.

When a naming part tells about more than one, do not add **s** to the verb.

Dogs **bark** their morning song.

Write a verb in each sentence. Make sure that the verb agrees with the naming part.

A duck quacks its morning song.

A frog _____ its morning song.

Frogs _____ their morning song.

A hen _____ its morning song.

Bears _____ their morning song.

Changing *y* to *i*

When the naming part of a sentence tells about one, add **s** to the verb. If the verb ends with a consonant plus **y**, change **y** to **i**. Then add **es**.

Tom and Tina **carry** the fishing rods.
Dad **carries** a basket, too.

Guided Practice

Write each verb in ( ) correctly.

1. Mom (study) the map before going to the lake.

2. Mom (copy) the map onto a sheet of paper.

3. Tom (hurry) to get ready on time.

4. Tina (carry) the sandwiches to the car.

5. Tom (try) to put the fishing rods in the trunk.

Independent Practice

Write each verb in ( ) correctly.

6. Dad (carry) the fishing rods to the lake.

7. Mom (try) to catch some fish.

8. Tina (study) the animals by the lake.

9. Tom (copy) his sister, and they both watch.

10. A frog (hurry) out of the water.

11. The frog (spy) some bugs.

12. The bugs (fly) away.

13. Two birds (dry) their feathers in the sun.

14. One bird (cry) when it sees a worm.

15. The worm (bury) itself in the ground.

)))) Writing Connection

Writing a Paragraph Draw a picture of an animal and write a paragraph about it. Use some of these verbs.

carry   hurry   dry   try   cry   fly

Use the spell-check on your computer to help you check that you spelled the verbs correctly.

Writing Contractions

A **contraction** is a short way to write two words. In a contraction, one or more letters are left out. An **apostrophe** (') is a mark that takes the place of the missing letters.

are + not *= aren't*   can + not *= can't*

The seeds **aren't** sprouting.
The seeds **can't** grow in the snow.

Guided Practice

Write the contraction for the underlined words.

1. The snow <u>has</u> <u>not</u> stopped.

2. Eva <u>can</u> <u>not</u> go outside.

3. The weather <u>is</u> <u>not</u> good.

4. Eva <u>did</u> <u>not</u> want to get wet.

5. She <u>could</u> <u>not</u> check the seeds she planted.

Independent Practice

Write the contraction for the underlined words.

6. The seeds <u>have</u> <u>not</u> grown in the garden.

7. They <u>did not</u> get enough sun.

8. Eva <u>had</u> <u>not</u> planted them correctly.

9. The seeds <u>were</u> <u>not</u> in a good spot.

10. The soil <u>was</u> <u>not</u> warm enough.

11. Eva <u>is</u> <u>not</u> happy.

12. She <u>did</u> <u>not</u> think this would happen.

13. Eva <u>should</u> <u>not</u> feel sad.

14. Eva <u>does not</u> want this to happen again.

15. She <u>can</u> <u>not</u> wait to plant other seeds.

))) Writing Connection

Giving Reasons Write a few sentences to explain why you think you shouldn't plant seeds in cold, dark places. Use some contractions in your sentences.

To type an apostrophe, push the " key.

Extra Practice

**Write each present-tense verb in ( )
correctly.**

1. Mario and Luz (copy) their
   science homework.

2. Luz (study) the weather.

3. Mario (want) to learn about sunflowers.

4. He (bury) some seeds in the soil.

5. Luz (help) him.

6. They (try) to grow sunflowers in winter!

**Write a contraction for the
underlined words.**

7. It <u>has</u> <u>not</u> snowed today.

8. Luz thinks the weather <u>was</u> <u>not</u>
   cold enough.

9. It <u>did</u> <u>not</u> rain either.

10. The temperature <u>is</u> <u>not</u> high.

Language Play

Act It Out

- Work with a small group. Sit in a circle.
- Think of ways animals move and sound.
- The first person says a sentence that tells how one animal moves or sounds.
- The next person says a sentence that tells how two of one kind of animal move or sound.
- Keep going around the circle until everyone has had at least two chances to say a sentence.

Writing Connection

Do and Don't Chart Make a chart that shows classroom rules. Think about what you should do. Then think about what you should not do. Write these rules in your Do and Don't Chart.

Classroom Rules	
Do	**Don't**
1. Raise your hand if you want to speak. 2. Keep your desk clean.	1. Don't talk out of turn.

TAAS PREP

Chapter Review

STANDARDIZED
TEST PREP

Choose the best answer for each underlined word.

1. The children <u>travel</u> to the mountain.

   a. travels

   b. traveling

   c. traveles

   d. correct as is

2. Alec <u>study</u> the tracks in the snow.

   a. studies

   b. studys

   c. study's

   d. correct as is

3. His friends <u>plays</u> in the snow.

   a. plaies

   b. playes

   c. play

   d. correct as is

4. Maria <u>trys</u> to pick up some snow.

   a. try

   b. tries

   c. tryes

   d. correct as is

5. She <u>doesn't</u> wear gloves.

   a. do'nt

   b. doesnt

   c. don't

   d. correct as is

6. Snow <u>melt</u> in her hands.

   a. melts

   b. melt's

   c. melties

   d. correct as is

Visit our website for more activities on using verbs correctly:

www.harcourtschool.com

▪ Study Skills ▪

Using an Atlas

An **atlas** is a book of maps. An atlas of the United States shows maps of all the states in the country. It may show where cities and bodies of water are. Look in the Table of Contents or the Index to help you find the map you need.

This map is like one you can find in an atlas.

Practice

Use the map of Texas to answer the questions.

1. Why do you think Austin has a star by it?

2. Which city is closest to Dallas?

3. What body of water is Corpus Christi near?

4. Which city is farthest west?

5. Imagine that you have an atlas of maps of the United States that are listed in alphabetical order. Would you look near the beginning, middle, or end to find a map of Texas?

Giving Examples

A **book report** tells what a book is about. It names the title and the author of the book. Then it tells who the characters are and what they do.

In a book report a writer tells what he or she thinks about a book. The writer may also include **examples**, or descriptions of parts of the book. Examples can show what a writer means or why a writer thinks a certain way.

Read this book report. What is the book about? What does the writer think about the book? Why?

Dear Mr. Blueberry
SIMON JAMES

<u>Dear Mr. Blueberry</u>
by Simon James

This book is about a girl named Emily and her teacher, Mr. Blueberry. Emily thinks that a whale is living in her pond. She writes letters to Mr. Blueberry and asks him questions about her whale. Emily and Mr. Blueberry write many letters to each other.

I like this book because it is unusual. The whole book is letters that the characters write. I also learned a lot about whales. I learned that whales live in salt water and eat tiny animals. You will like this book if you like whales.

If a book has an illustrator as well as an author, write the illustrator's name under the author's name. You may even want to tell about the book's art in your report. Remember to include examples in your writing about the art.

Think About It

1. What does the writer tell about in the first paragraph of the book report? What does the writer tell about in the second paragraph?

2. Do you think you would like this book? Use examples from the book report to tell why or why not.

Writer's Craft

Giving Examples

Examples show what the writer means.

> I like this book because it is unusual. *The whole book is letters.*

The writer could have said only that the book is unusual. The second sentence tells **why** it is unusual.

> I also learned a lot about whales. *I learned that whales live in salt water and eat tiny animals.*

The writer could have said only that he or she learned a lot about whales. The second sentence gives an example of **what** the writer learned.

A. Give an example to support each idea below. Use the Idea Bank to help you.

1. This book is good.
2. The movie is funny.
3. That board game is fun.
4. The show was boring.

Idea Bank

- **There was no action in the first half.**
- **The main character has an exciting adventure in space.**
- **My whole family can play it together.**
- **The main character tells a funny joke about an apple.**

B. Reread "Jalapeño Bagels," on pages 366–372. Then give examples from the story to complete this book report.

Jalapeño Bagels
by Natasha Wing

"Jalapeño Bagels" is about a boy named Pablo. He is trying to choose a food for his class's International Day. Pablo goes to his parents' bakery. At the bakery, Pablo helps his parents make many treats, such as 1. _____. The 2. _____ look especially good.

I like this book because the foods are interesting. For example, I think it is interesting how Pablo makes 3. _____. I also think the part about 4. _____ _____ is interesting because 5. _____. You will like this book if you like food.

Writing and Thinking

Reflect Tell what helped you think of examples. Write your ideas. Share your ideas in a small group.

Applying the Craft TAAS PREP

Read this student book report. Think about how the examples show what the writer means.

<u>Abuela</u> —————————— title

by Arthur Dorros —————————— author

<u>Abuela</u> is about a girl named Rosalba and her grandma. They have imaginary adventures in the city. Rosalba imagines that they fly all over the city. ⎤ what the book is about

This is a good story because of Rosalba's imagination. I like the part where they fly around the top of the Statue of Liberty and hang on to the tail of an airplane. I think you will like this book if you like imaginary adventures. — examples / what the writer thinks about the book

Looking at the Model

1. Which example best shows what the writer means? Explain.

2. How do these examples make this book report better?

Your Turn

Write a book report about a book you have read. Be sure to give examples that show what you mean.

Prewriting and Drafting

STEP 1 **Develop your ideas.**

Ask yourself these questions.

- Why do I like or not like this book?
- What examples can I give to support my ideas?
- What can I tell my readers to make them want to read this book or not want to read it?

STEP 2 **Brainstorm examples.**

Make a chart. Write examples that tell why you did or did not like the book.

About My Book

Title _____

Author _____

Please check correct box.

☐ I liked this book.

☐ I did not like this book.

Give two examples why you did or did not like the book. _____

_____

_____

STEP 3 **Write your draft.**

Use your chart and What Good Writers Do to write a draft of your book report.

What Good Writers Do

☑ Remember to use examples to show your readers why you think a certain way.

☑ Plan your ideas.

Editing Your Book Report

Share your draft with a few classmates. Together, think about how you can make your book report better. Use the checklist and the Editor's Marks to help you revise your book report.

 My book report tells the title of the book and the author's name.

 My book report tells what I think about the book. I give examples that show why I think this way.

Sharing with Others

Meet with a partner or a small group. Share your book report. Read it aloud.

•Handwriting•

Forming Letters Correctly

Follow these tips to make sure your letters are formed correctly.

- Make smooth curves. Close up circle letters.
- Make straight lines correctly.
- Form letters made up of curves and straight lines correctly.
- Make slanted lines correctly.

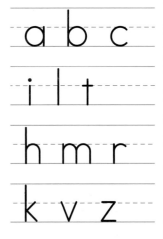

Practice

Write these letters. Use your best handwriting. Follow the tips. Use the Handwriting Models on page 490 to help you.

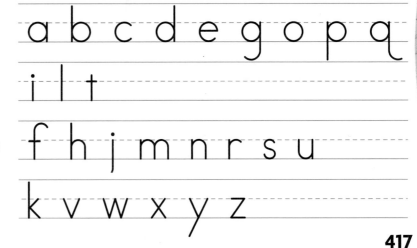

curves

straight lines

combination

slanted lines

Fixing "And Then" Sentences

Read the cartoon.

Bobby's Long Weekend...

Hi, Bobby. How was your weekend?

It was great, Eric!

I went to the new science museum. And then I took a tour. And then I saw a real lizard.

Neat! I...

And then I saw a movie about the planets. And then I met a real astronaut. And then I went to the gift shop.

And then I got four marvelous books. And then I went home and read all the books...

THE END

Tell about things that Bobby did at the museum in the order in which they happened. This time use the time-order words *first*, *next*, *then*, and *last* instead of the words *and then*.

Time-order words help tell about the order in which things happen. Use time-order words instead of the words *and then* to tell what happened.

First I went to the new science museum.
Next I took a tour and saw a real lizard.

Write the paragraph using time-order words.

Last weekend I helped my grandmother in her garden. I dug a hole in the ground. And then I put in some seeds. And then we covered them up with dirt. And then we watered them.

Writing Longer Sentences

You can combine two short sentences
to make one longer sentence.

Combine naming parts.

Children go home. **Parents** go home.
Children and **parents** go home.

Combine telling parts.

The children **talk**. The children **laugh**.
The children **talk** and **laugh**.

Combine other words.

The museum is **big**. The museum is **bright**.
The museum is **big** and **bright**.

Guided Practice

Combine each set of sentences.

1. A smart guide meets Ms. Li.
   A smart guide meets the class.

2. Susan asks to see a snake.
   Jeff asks to see a snake.

3. The guide points to a cage.
   The guide reads the sign.

Independent Practice

Combine each set of sentences.

4. The snake is small.
   The snake is green.

5. The snake crawls in the cage.
   The snake drinks in the cage.

6. The teachers look at a poster.
   The parents look at a poster.

7. They see photos of Jupiter.
   They see photos of Mars.

8. Jupiter is a large planet.
   Jupiter is a colorful planet.

9. The children ask questions.
   The children take pictures.

10. The children line up quietly to go home.
    The children line up quickly to go home.

Writing Connection

Revising Find a piece of writing in your Writing Portfolio. Revise sentences that you can combine.

Use cut and paste on your computer to help combine your sentences.

Using a Series Comma

Sometimes a series of three or more nouns, verbs, or adjectives is used in a sentence. Put a comma (,) between the items in a series.

Peter, Judy, Joe, and Carol share a table.
The children draw, paint, and write about the museum.
They use red, yellow, and blue paint.

Guided Practice

Write each sentence correctly using the series comma.

1. Carol shares crayons with Peter Judy and Joe.

2. Joe traces draws and colors with pencils.

3. Judy writes a story about a small lonely sad planet.

4. The planet is happy when he meets Earth Mars and Jupiter.

5. He smiles laughs and plays with his new friends.

422

 **Remember** **Put a comma (,) between the items in a series.**

Independent Practice

Write each sentence correctly using the series comma.

6. Next they read study and color a map of the planets.

7. Mercury Venus Earth and Mars are closest to the sun.

8. The largest planets are Jupiter Saturn Neptune and Uranus.

9. The children learn that stars are bright hot and large.

10. Then they plan draw and color their own maps.

11. They put stars planets and a comet on their maps.

12. Dan's map shows the Little Dipper the Big Dipper and the sun.

Writing Connection

Description Brainstorm words that describe you. Then write three sentences about yourself. Be sure to use commas correctly.

Use your computer to add any missing commas to your writing.

Extra Practice

**Write each paragraph using
time-order words.**

1.　We all get teeth the same way. Small teeth
grow in when we are babies. And then the
baby teeth fall out. And then adult teeth
grow in. And then those teeth replace the
baby teeth.

2.　How does a caterpillar become a butterfly?
The caterpillar hatches out of an egg. And
then it eats so it can grow. And then its body
turns into a shell. And then it breaks out of
the shell and is a beautiful butterfly.

**Combine the short sentences to make
one longer sentence.**

3. Butterfly eggs can be green.
　 Butterfly eggs can be orange.

4. Caterpillars hatch on leaves.
　 Caterpillars crawl on leaves.

Write the list in each sentence correctly.

5. Caterpillars eat beans fruit leaves and
　 other plants.

6. Caterpillars live in cold hot or warm places.

Make It Longer

- Play this game with four people. Form two teams.
- Make cards with sets of three verbs, adjectives, and nouns.
- Pick a card. Work with your partner to make up a sentence that uses all three words on the card.
- The next team does the same thing with a different card.
- Play until all the cards are gone. You get one point for each correct sentence.

dogs cats
mice

act speak
write

excited
happy
proud

Writing Connection

Sales Poster Think about a store you have visited. Make a poster that will help sell items in the store. Name and describe the items so that they sound interesting. Use lists of items in your sentences.

Pat's Art Store on Smith Street has markers, pencils, and crayons.

Walk, run, or drive down to catch the great sales now!

Chapter Review STANDARDIZED TEST PREP

Read each numbered item. Choose the best answer.

1. Ms. Kim told the class about a trip. Then they cheered.

    a. Ms. Kim told the class about a trip they cheered.

    b. And then Ms. Kim told the class about a trip. Then they cheered.

    c. correct as is

2. First they will take a tour of the museum. Then they will eat.

    a. First they will take a tour of the museum. And then they will eat.

    b. Last they will take a tour of the museum. And then they will eat.

    c. correct as is

3. Donna, Sam and Trish like dinosaurs.

    a. Donna, Sam, and Trish like dinosaurs.

    b. Donna Sam and Trish like dinosaurs.

    c. correct as is

4. One dinosaur is black green, red.

    a. One dinosaur is black green and red.

    b. One dinosaur is black, green, and red.

    c. correct as is

Visit our website for more activities about fixing sentence problems:
www.harcourtschool.com

◼ Vocabulary ◼

Suffixes TAAS SKILL

> A **suffix** is a group of letters added to the end of a word. A suffix changes the meaning of a word.
>
> | Suffix | Meaning | Words |
> |--------|---------|-------|
> | – less | without | useless, careless |
> | – ful | full of | useful, careful |

Practice

Add *-ful* or *-less* to the word in ( ). Write the new sentence.

1. Reggie cleaned the chalkboard to be (help).

2. He dropped the chalk because he was (care).

3. A small piece of broken chalk is (use).

4. His teacher asked him to be more (care).

5. Reggie was (thank) she was not angry.

Spelling Words That Sound Alike

Read the poem.

Giraffes

I like them.
Ask me why.

Because they hold their heads so high.
Because their necks stretch to the sky.
Because they're quiet, calm, and shy.
Because they run so fast they fly.
Because their eyes are velvet brown.
Because their coats are spotted tan.
Because they eat the tops of trees.
Because their legs have knobby knees.
Because
Because
Because. That's why
I like giraffes.

Mary Ann Hoberman

Vocabulary Power

scamper

Talk about your favorite animals. Use *they're* and *their* to tell why you like them.

Some words sound the same but have different meanings and spellings.

The giraffes are over **there** by the trees.
Their legs are long and thin.
They're nibbling on the leaves.

Write about another animal to add more lines to the poem.

I like ____________.

because they're ____________.

because they're ____________.

because their ____________.

because their ____________.

Because

Because

Because. That's why

I like ____________.

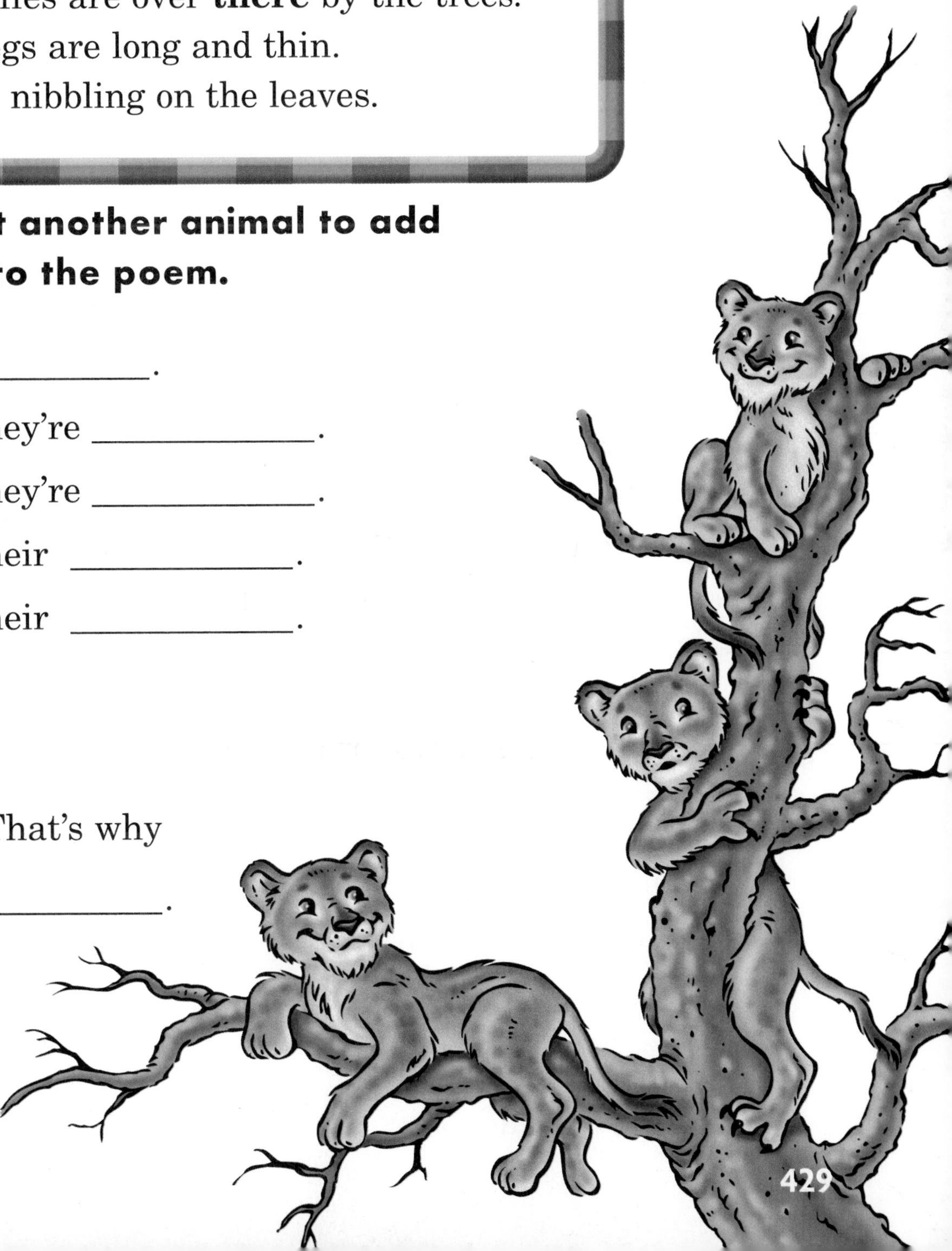

Using *there*, *their*, and *they're*

Some words sound alike but have different meanings and spellings.

Word	Meaning
their	belonging to them
there	that place
they're	contraction for *they are*

The Smiths planned **their** trip to New York.
Then a big snowstorm hit **there**.
Now **they're** planning another trip.

Guided Practice

Write *their*, *there*, or *they're* to complete each sentence.

1. On _____ trip they will go to Texas.

2. The family will see many things _____.

3. The children are excited about _____ plane ride.

4. _____ bags are on board.

5. _____ all ready to go.

Independent Practice

Write *their*, *there*, or *they're* to complete each sentence.

6. _____ leaving the airport.

7. They get to _____ hotel.

8. The maps are over _____.

9. _____ tour bus takes them to the river walk.

10. The children like the sights _____.

11. Now _____ hungry.

12. A restaurant is over _____ by the river.

13. They get _____ meals quickly.

14. At the end of the day, _____ tired.

15. _____ trip was fun.

Writing Connection

Write About Classmates Think about yourself and a group of classmates. Write three sentences about how they are like you. Use *they're*, *there*, or *their* in the sentences. Draw a picture.

Use your computer to help you write your sentences.

Using *to*, *too*, and *two*

The words **to**, **too**, and **two** sound the same but have different spellings and meanings.

Word	Meaning
to	in the direction of
too	also
two	one more than one

Ken walks **to** Pat's house.
Maya walks there, **too**.
The **two** of them walk together.

Guided Practice

Choose *to*, *too*, or *two* to complete each sentence.

1. Sometimes Kevin and Pat walk (to, too, two) the park.

2. Once they heard (to, too, two) kittens.

3. A police officer heard them, (to, too, two).

4. They all ran (to, too, two) see what was the problem.

5. The kittens were stuck on (to, too, two) high tree branches.

Remember *To*, *too*, and *two* sound the same, but have different spellings and meanings.

Independent Practice

Choose *to*, *too*, or *two* to complete each sentence.

6. Other officers came (to, too, two) the park.

7. Many people were watching, (to, too, two).

8. A fire truck showed up, (to, too, two).

9. Firefighters brought a tall ladder (to, too, two) the tree.

10. The ladder had (to, too, two) cracks in it.

11. Luckily, the truck had (to, too, two) ladders.

12. The other ladder was tall, (to, too, two).

13. (To, Too, Two) officers carried it to the tree.

14. The (to, too, two) kittens were saved!

15. The boys went (to, too, two) see them.

Writing Connection

Listen for Troublesome Words Write three sentences. Use *to*, *too*, or *two* in them. Read the sentences to a classmate. Ask the classmate to write the correct troublesome words.

Use your computer to edit your sentences for *to*, *too*, and *two*.

Extra Practice

**Write *their*, *there*, or *they're* to complete
each sentence.**

1. It is raining out _____ at the lake.

2. Most children bring _____ raincoats.

3. _____ going to sail anyway.

4. The sails are raised on the boats over
   _____.

5. Now _____ ready to go.

**Choose *to*, *too*, or *two* to complete
each sentence.**

6. The class went (to, too, two) the dock.

7. (To, Too, Two) boats sailed away.

8. A motorboat went out, (to, too, two).

9. The (to, too, two) sails on each boat
   filled with air.

10. The boats sailed (to, too, two) the
    other side of the lake.

Language Play

Which Word?

- Take turns with a partner.
- Pick a word from the list.
  Do not tell your partner
  what the word is.
- Say a sentence using the word.
- Have your partner write the word.
- Score one point for each word written correctly.
  The first player with 5 points wins.

to	there
too	their
two	they're

Writing Connection

Tongue Twister Tongue twisters are fun to say because many of their words begin with the same sound. Write some tongue twisters using troublesome words. Then try reading them aloud. How fast can you read them and still say each word correctly?

Tongue Twisters

Their three friends think they're thrifty.

Tori wore two shoes to town, too.

They're thirsty and their throats throb.

Chapter Review

Choose the best answer for each underlined word.

1. <u>They're</u> is the cave.

    a. There

    b. Their

    c. correct as is

2. Go in with <u>to</u> people.

    a. two

    b. too

    c. correct as is

3. You can't go <u>two</u> the cave alone.

    a. too

    b. to

    c. correct as is

4. The rangers follow <u>their</u> own rule.

    a. they're

    b. there

    c. correct as is

5. <u>They're</u> never alone in the cave.

    a. There

    b. Their

    c. correct as is

6. You have to follow the rule, <u>to</u>.

    a. too

    b. two

    c. correct as is

**Visit our website
for more activities
with troublesome words**
www.harcourtschool.com

436

◼ Technology ◼

Using a Computer to Get Information

You can use a computer's search engine to help you find information. A search engine is a computer's tool for finding different information. Picture **1** shows how to search using a key word. A **key word** tells what your topic is. Type a key word and click on Go. Picture **2** shows a guided search. You click on key word choices on the computer screen.

1

Search by Word

Search for: dinosaurs   **Go**

2

Guided Search

Choose subject: Science
Choose grade: 2
Choose key word: Dinosaurs
Words G-L
Words M-R
Words S-Z
No key word
Go

Practice

Write the key word you would use to find answers to each question.

1. What is the biggest city in Texas?

2. How do clouds form?

3. What does a veterinarian do?

A research report gives information about a topic. Each paragraph has a main idea and detail sentences that tell more about the topic. As you read this report, think about its main ideas.

Award-Winning Author and Illustrator

You're Aboard Spaceship Earth

by Patricia Lauber

ILLUSTRATED BY HOLLY KELLER

Water on Earth

Earth has had the same water for billions of years. Plants, animals, and people all use it. Yet Earth doesn't run out of water, because the same water is used over and over again. It is recycled.

439

Most of our water comes from the oceans. Water is drawn into the air by the sun's heat. It becomes a gas called water vapor. Salt from the ocean water is left behind.

WATER VAPOR

RAIN

Water vapor forms clouds. Rain clouds drop their water on the earth. Some of it falls in the oceans. Some falls on land. There much of the rainwater runs off into streams. The streams flow into rivers. The rivers flow back into the oceans.

Again the sun's heat draws water out of the oceans. Water vapor forms clouds. It falls again as rain.

Water is used in many ways. The roots of plants draw water from the soil. Animals drink water and bathe in it. So do people.

Rushing water can be put to work. It can turn machines that make electricity. Paper mills use water. Other factories do too.

Tugs and barges travel on rivers. So do canoes and rowboats.

Water fills swimming pools. Heated, it warms buildings in cold weather. It washes clothes, dishes, and cars.

How many other uses can you think of?

After being used, water goes back into the oceans, is drawn into the air, and falls again as rain. Some of the rain that falls on you probably fell on the dinosaurs.

Think About It

1. What is the most interesting thing you found out about water? Read the sentences that tell about it to a partner.

2. What are some of the uses of water? Why is water important to you?

Parts of a Research Report

A research report gives information on a **topic**. The report's **title** tells what the topic is.

Within the report there may be one or more paragraphs. Each paragraph has one **main idea** and sentences that give **details** about the main idea.

Write the main idea shown. It is from the paragraph on page 442. Reread the paragraph. Write details from that paragraph in a list. Then do the same thing with another paragraph in the report.

Topic: Water on Earth

Main Idea:
Water is used in many ways.

Detail:

Detail:

Detail:

Main Idea:
Detail:

Detail:

A Student Model

Jermaine enjoyed reading about how water is used on Earth. He wrote a report about another topic in which he is interested. Read his report, and think about its parts.

Dinosaurs

Dinosaurs lived millions of years ago. The first dinosaurs lived about 245 million years ago. The last dinosaurs died about 65 million years ago. No one is sure why this happened.

Many different kinds of dinosaurs roamed the Earth. Tyrannosaurus rex was big and fierce and weighed more than 1,400 pounds. Stegosaurus had bony plates on its back. Troodon weighed less than 100 pounds, but some scientists think it was one of the smartest dinosaurs.

The **title** tells the topic, or what the report is about.

The **main idea** answers an important question about the topic.

The **details** are examples that tell about the main idea.

Looking at the Model

1. What is the title of Jermaine's report?

2. What is the topic of the report? Why do you think Jermaine chose that topic?

3. When did dinosaurs live? Why did they die out?

4. What is the main idea of the second paragraph? What kinds of dinosaurs does Jermaine write about?

Writer's Craft

Giving Examples

Jermaine used examples to help you understand his main ideas. Find the examples in Jermaine's report.

- What kinds of dinosaurs does Jermaine name?

- How much did Tyrannosaurus weigh?

- What did Stegosaurus look like?

- What kind of dinosaur was Troodon?

Prewriting

Before Jermaine wrote his report, he made a list of topics that interested him. He also thought about his classmates who would read the report. Jermaine knows they like dinosaurs. He decided to write about dinosaurs.

Next Jermaine thought about what he wanted to know about dinosaurs. He wrote each idea as a question on a note card.

Then Jermaine went to the library to find answers to his questions. He read books and used a computer to find information. He wrote the answers on the note cards.

> When did dinosaurs live?
> • The last dinosaur died about 65 million years ago.
> • The first dinosaur lived about 245 million years ago.
> • No one knows for sure why they died.

Jermaine put his note cards in an order that made sense. He used the cards to write an outline. An **outline** shows the order of main ideas and details in a piece of writing.

Dinosaurs Outline

1. When did dinosaurs live?

    a. last dinosaur, 65 million years ago

    b. first dinosaur, 245 million years ago

    c. No one knows why they died.

2. What kinds of dinosaurs were there?

    a. Tyrannosaurus rex

    b. Stegosaurus

    c. Troodon

When did dinosaurs live?

- The last dinosaur died about 65 million years ago.

- The first dinosaur lived about 245 million years ago.

- No one knows for sure why they died.

Your Turn

STEP 1 Think of interesting topics.
Make a list of topics you think are interesting and would like to know more about.

STEP 2 Choose one topic. Think about who will read your report. Pick a topic.

STEP 3 Use note cards. Write each question you want to answer on a note card.

STEP 4 Use your note cards to write an outline. Put the cards in an order that makes sense. Then write an outline. The questions are the main ideas. The answers are the details about the main ideas.

Use your computer to help organize your notes.

Drafting

Jermaine used his outline and notes to help him write a first draft. He used the first question and its answers for the first paragraph. He used the second question and its answers for the second paragraph.

Jermaine wrote in the first draft the most important things he found out. He knew he could add more details later. Read Jermaine's first draft.

Dinosaurs

Dinosaurs lived millions of years ago. The last dinosaurs died about 65 million years ago. The first dinosaurs lived about 245 million years ago.

Many different kinds of dinosaurs roamed the Earth. Tyrannosaurus rex was big and fierce. Stegosaurus had plates on its back. Troodon

Look at Jermaine's outline and notes. What other details could he add to the report?

Dinosaurs Outline

1. When did dinosaurs live?

    a. last dinosaur, 65 million years ago

    b. first dinosaur, 245 million years ago

    c. No one knows why they died.

2. What kinds of dinosaurs were there?

    a. Tyrannosaurus rex

    b. Stegosaurus

    c. Troodon

When did dinosaurs live?
- The last dinosaur died about 65 million years ago.
- The first dinosaur lived about 245 million years ago.
- No one knows for sure why they died.

What Good Writers Do

✓ Follow your outline to write the first draft.

✓ Don't worry about mistakes. You can fix them later.

**Your Turn**

Use your notes, outline, and What Good Writers Do to write a draft of your research report.

Double-space your draft so you have room to mark changes on your printout.

Revising

Jermaine and a partner talked about how to make the draft better. Then Jermaine added details. He also changed the order of some sentences to make the information clearer.

DRAFT

Dinosaurs

Dinosaurs lived millions of years ago. The last dinosaurs died about 65 million years ago. The first dinosaurs lived about 245 million years ago. No one is sure why this happened.

Many different kinds of dinosaurs roamed the Earth. Tyrannosaurus rex was big and fierce *and weighed more than 1,400 pounds*. Stegosaurus had *bony* plates on its back. Troodon wayed less than 100 pounds, but some scientists thinks it were one of the smartest dinosaurs.

What Good Writers Do

 Decide if your writing is clear. Do you need to change any sentences?

 Can you add details to tell more about your topic?

Editor's Marks

 Add.

 Change.

 Take out.

 Move.

Your Turn

Talk with a partner about how your draft could be better. Use What Good Writers Do and the Editor's Marks to make changes.

Proofreading

Jermaine read his report once more to look for mistakes. Why did Jermaine make each change in red?

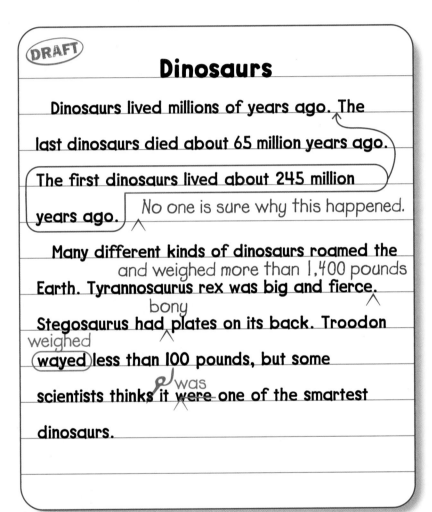

DRAFT

Dinosaurs

Dinosaurs lived millions of years ago. The last dinosaurs died about 65 million years ago. The first dinosaurs lived about 245 million years ago. No one is sure why this happened.

Many different kinds of dinosaurs roamed the and weighed more than 1,400 pounds Earth. Tyrannosaurus rex was big and fierce. bony Stegosaurus had plates on its back. Troodon weighed wayed less than 100 pounds, but some was scientists thinks it were one of the smartest dinosaurs.

What Good Writers Do

 Make sure each verb agrees with the subject.

 Be sure each sentence begins with a capital letter and ends with an end mark.

 Check your spelling. Look up words that sound alike.

Editor's Marks

 Check the spelling.

 Change.

 Take out.

Your Turn

Now read your story once more. Use What Good Writers Do and the Editor's Marks to fix any mistakes.

Use your computer's spell-check to help you find any spelling mistakes.

Publishing

Jermaine made a clean copy of his report. He also drew pictures of dinosaurs and labeled them to show some of the information.

Your Turn

Write your report neatly on a clean sheet of paper. Make the changes. Use a computer if you like. Here are some more publishing ideas.

- **Make a magazine-style article.**
  Type your report on your computer. Then make drawings or find photos for the report. Add them to your report by using Cut and Paste or by scanning them. Write a caption for each one.

- **Make a poster report.**
  Draw pictures that show information from your report. Arrange and glue them on a poster. Then write a caption for each picture. Attach a copy of the report to the poster.

Add your finished research report to your Writing Portfolio.

Dinosaurs
— of Long Ago —

Dinosaurs lived millions of years ago. The first dinosaurs lived about 245 million years ago. The last dinosaurs died about 65 million years ago. No one is sure why this happened.

Many different kinds of dinosaurs roamed the Earth. Tyrannosaurus rex was big and fierce and weighed more than 1,400 pounds. Stegosaurus had bony plates on its back.

Troodon weighed less than 100 pounds, but some scientists think it was one of the smartest dinosaurs.

Listening and Speaking

Giving an Oral Report

You can give an oral report on research you have done. Practice these tips.

Tips for Oral Reports

- Make drawings, charts, or models. Point to the pictures and models to help explain.
- Use notes to give your report. When you speak, look at your notes and then at your classmates.
- Speak slowly and clearly.
- Speak loudly enough so everyone can hear you.

Practice these tips when listening to a report.

Listening Tips

- Listen for the topic.
- Take notes to help you sum up and remember main ideas.
- Listen for details.
- Write down questions you have. Ask the questions after the report is given.

Unit 6
Grammar Review
pages 392-433

Noun-Pronoun Agreement pages 392-393
Write the pronoun that agrees with the underlined noun in each set of sentences.

1. The <u>children</u> look outside. _____ are surprised.

2. <u>Snow</u> fell last night. _____ is a foot deep.

3. <u>Ann</u> can't wait. _____ gets her snowsuit.

Word Order for Pronouns pages 394-395
Write the correct words in ( ) to complete each sentence.

4. Ed calls (Ted and me, me and Ted) early.

5. (Ted and I, I and Ted) will help Ed study snow.

Changing *y* to *i* pages 402-403
Write each verb in ( ) correctly.

6. Ed and Ann (hurry) over to meet us.

7. Ted (try) to take a picture of a snowflake.

Writing Contractions pages 404-405
Write the contraction for the underlined words.

8. Rosa and Tom <u>can not</u> go outside.

9. They <u>are not</u> ready.

10. Rosa <u>has not</u> finished her breakfast.

Writing Longer Sentences pages 420–421

Combine each set of sentences.

11. The children saw tracks.
    The parents saw tracks.

12. We saw deer.
    We saw rabbits.

Using a Series Comma pages 422–423

Write each sentence correctly using the series comma.

13. Bears beavers and turtles sleep all winter.

14. Deer eat roots berries and any other food they can find.

Using *there*, *their*, and *they're* pages 430–431

Write *there*, *their*, or *they're* to complete each sentence.

15. The children are over _____.

16. _____ having fun in the snow.

17. Are they all wearing _____ hats?

Using *to*, *too*, and *two* pages 432–433

Write *to*, *too*, or *two* to complete each sentence.

18. Ted and I go _____ the ice-skating rink.

19. Ann and Ed want to go, _____.

20. We are all going to skate at _____ o'clock.

Social Studies

Safe Summer Fun

Summer is almost here, and you will do many things outdoors. While you are having fun, you need to stay safe. Make a class book of summer safety tips to get ready for summer fun.

Plan Your Book

- Brainstorm a list of things you might do and places you might go this summer. Then sort the items into shorter lists for chapters in your book. For example, *pool* and *beach* may go into the "safe swimming" chapter.

- Write questions about safety for each item in every chapter. Then find answers to your safety questions. Look in books, use your computer, and talk to people such as lifeguards.

- Write the answers on note cards. Use the note cards to help you write an outline.

Write and Publish Your Book

- Use your outline and notes to write your chapters. Then revise and proofread them.

- If a chapter will have pictures, make sketches to show what will be in each one.

- Write a clean copy of your book. Use a computer if you want. Make a title page, a table of contents, and a cover for your book.

- Use your sketches to make final drawings. Add them to your chapters.

- Make copies of your book for classmates and your family members.

Books to Read

Willie Takes a Hike
by Gloria Rand
Fiction
Willie, a mouse, learns how important it is to be prepared when he takes a hike.
Award-Winning Author

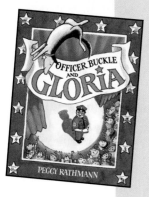

Officer Buckle and Gloria
by Peggy Rathmann
Fantasy
A police dog named Gloria helps a police officer give safety tips to children.
Caldecott Medal

Cumulative Review

Units 1–6

Unit 1: All About Sentences

Sentences pages 24–29, 36–37

Write each group of words to make a sentence. Then circle the naming part. Underline the telling part.

1. to store the goes Lian
2. a book buys she
3. about an owl the book is
4. in tree a lives the owl

Combining Parts of Sentences pages 38–39

Use *and* to join each pair of sentences. Write the new sentence.

5. Kate went to the park. Sam went to the park.
6. Eric played with them. I played with them.
7. The trees were pretty. The flowers were pretty.

Unit 2: All About Nouns

Nouns pages 96–97, 124–125

Write each sentence. Underline each noun. Write if it is a person, place, animal, or thing.

8. My family is at the zoo.
9. Seals are playing in the water.
10. A girl feeds the seals some food.
11. My sister pets an elephant.

Using Possessive Nouns pages 100–101

Use 's to rewrite the underlined words.

12. <u>The ball of the dog</u> is under the chair.

13. My game is in <u>the room of my brother</u>.

14. <u>The computer of Emily</u> is easy to use.

Using *He, She, It,* and *They* pages 136–137

Write each sentence. Use a pronoun for the underlined words.

15. <u>My sister Julie</u> gave me a puzzle.

16. <u>The puzzle</u> has many pieces.

17. <u>John</u> puts some pieces together.

18. <u>My friends</u> help me, too.

Unit 3: Verbs

Using the Correct Verb pages 172–173, 202–203

Write the correct verb to finish each sentence.

19. Three deer (was, were) feeding in the field.

20. Some rabbits (hop, hops) nearby.

21. A fox (chase, chases) one of the rabbits.

22. The rabbit (was, were) faster than the fox.

Adding *ed* to Verbs pages 182–185

Rewrite each sentence. Write the verb in ( ) to tell about the past.

23. We (look) for shells along the beach.

24. Rico (collect) four colorful shells.

25. Suddenly, one of the shells (move)!

Unit 4: All About Adjectives

Adjectives pages 244–245, 254–255, 272–273

Choose an adjective from the box to complete each sentence. Write each sentence.

sour	leafy	sweet	three	small	yellow

26. Joey has _____ lemons.

27. The lemons are _____.

28. Lemon juice has a _____ taste.

29. Lemons grow on _____ trees.

30. They come from _____ flowers.

31. Lemon flowers have a _____ smell.

Adding *er* and *est* pages 282–283

Write the correct adjective in ( ) to complete each sentence.

32. A robin is (shorter, shortest) than an owl.

33. A hummingbird is the (smaller, smallest) of all.

34. A hawk's beak is (sharper, sharpest) than a duck's.

35. An ostrich has the (longer, longest) legs of any bird.

Unit 5: More About Verbs

Using the Correct Verb pages 320–321, 330–331

Write the correct verb in ( ) to complete each sentence.

36. Last week, Dad (give, gave) me running shoes.

37. I (do, done) exercises before I run.

Joining Sentences pages 322–323

Use *and* to join the sentences. Remember to use a comma (,) before *and*.

38. Leon plays the piano. Sara plays the violin.

39. I liked the concert. Mary liked it, too.

40. They took a bow. The audience applauded.

Using Adverbs pages 358–359

Write the adverb in each sentence. Then write *how*, *when*, or *where* for each adverb.

41. The play begins soon.

42. It is exciting here.

43. The audience sits quietly.

Unit 6: Usage Wrap-Up

Noun–Pronoun Agreement pages 392–393

Write the pronoun that agrees with the underlined noun in each pair of sentences.

44. <u>Dad</u> looks out the window. _____ calls to us.

45. Look at those <u>bears</u>! _____ are brown bears.

46. One <u>bear</u> is larger. _____ is the mother bear.

Writing Contractions pages 404–405

Write the contraction for the underlined words.

47. Snakes <u>can not</u> walk or run.

48. Ostriches <u>do not</u> fly.

49. Whales <u>are not</u> fish.

Standardized Test Prep

Kinds of Sentences pages 54–55, 64–65

Read each sentence. Choose the answer that tells the kind of sentence it is.

50. We went shopping.

   a. question

   b. command

   c. statement

51. Do you like this store?

   a. question

   b. exclamation

   c. statement

52. What a great toy!

   a. question

   b. command

   c. exclamation

53. Pay the clerk.

   a. statement

   b. command

   c. exclamation

Using *Am*, *Is*, and *Are* pages 200–201

Choose the correct verb for each sentence.

54. The children _____ outside.

   a. am   **b.** is   **c.** are

55. I _____ collecting rocks.

   a. am   **b.** is   **c.** are

56. Tina _____ looking at plants.

   a. am   **b.** is   **c.** are

57. We _____ at nature camp.

   a. am   **b.** is   **c.** are

Using *Has*, *Have*, and *Had* pages 210–213

Choose the correct verb for each sentence.

58. Once I _____ a hamster.

   a. has   **b.** have   **c.** had

59. Now I _____ a dog.

   a. has   **b.** have   **c.** had

Choose the best answer for the underlined words.

60. Today is <u>July 21 2001</u>.

    a. July 21, 2001

    b. July, 21 2001

    c. correct as is

62. He will be back on <u>August 2, 2001</u>.

    a. August 2 2001

    b. August, 2, 2001

    c. correct as is

61. Dad is in <u>Tucson Arizona</u>.

    a. Tucson, Arizona

    b. Tucson, Arizona,

    c. correct as is

63. We live in <u>Bangor Maine</u>.

    a. Bangor, Maine

    b. Bangor, Maine,

    c. correct as is

Using *there, their,* and *they're* pages 430–431

Choose the correct word for each sentence.

64. Look at the birds over _____.

    a. there   **b.** their   **c.** they're

65. See _____ colorful feathers.

    a. there   **b.** their   **c.** they're

Using *to, too,* and *two* pages 432–433

Choose the correct word to complete each sentence.

66. Joe wants to go _____ the science fair.

    a. to   **b.** too   **c.** two

67. He has _____ free tickets for us.

    a. to   **b.** too   **c.** two

68. Loni wants to go, _____.

    a. to   **b.** too   **c.** two

Extra Practice

What Is a Sentence? pages 24–25

Write each group of words that is a sentence.

1. wants a puppy
2. Kim goes to the pet store.
3. The puppies play and bark.

Word Order in a Sentence pages 26–27
Beginning and Ending a Sentence pages 28–29

Write each group of words in an order that makes sense. Begin and end each sentence correctly.

4. one puppy Kim to runs
5. its little tail wags it
6. on the hand it licks Kim

Naming Parts and Telling Parts pages 36–37

Write each sentence. Circle the naming part. Underline the telling part.

7. Kim takes the puppy home.
8. The puppy plays with a ball.

Combining Parts of Sentences pages 38–39

Use *and* to join the pair of sentences. Write the sentence.

9. The puppy went to sleep. Kim went to sleep.

Using Statements and Questions   pages 54–55

Write each sentence correctly.

10. have you named your puppy

11. i call her Sadie

12. where did you get her

Sentences That Go Together   pages 56–57

Write the sentences that belong. Leave out the sentence that does not belong.

13.   I like my puppy, Sadie. We have a lot of fun. I give her food and water every day. My birthday is tomorrow. I take her for walks.

Exclamations and Commands   pages 64–65

Write each sentence correctly.

14. how funny puppies are

15. watch her chase the ball

16. give her a pat on the head

Using Different Kinds of Sentences   pages 66–67

Change each sentence into the kind of sentence shown in ( ). Write the new sentence.

17. I may play with your puppy. (question)

18. Would you throw the ball for her? (command)

Extra Practice

Nouns for People, Places, Animals, and Things pages 98–99

Write each sentence. Underline each noun that names a person, place, or thing.

1. The family lives next to the school.

2. They have a yard with a fence around it.

Using Possessive Nouns pages 100–101

Use 's to rewrite the underlined words.

3. The house of my friend is across the street.

4. I ride my bike to the store of Grandpa.

Making Nouns Plural pages 108–109

Write the noun in ( ) so it names more than one.

5. I saw several of my (friend).

6. I bought six (peach) at the market.

7. Two (bus) passed me on the street.

Plural Nouns That Change Spelling pages 110–111

Write the noun in ( ) to mean more than one.

8. Three (child) were playing in the park.

9. They had sneakers on their (foot).

10. Two (woman) said hello to me.

People, Places, and Animals pages 126–127

Write the proper noun in ( ) correctly. Then write if it is a person, a place, or an animal.

11. My neighbor (mario perez) has a dog.

12. His dog's name is (boxer).

13. Boxer came from (stony brook).

Days, Months, and Holidays pages 128–129

Write each proper noun correctly.

14. Our family went on vacation in may.

15. We came back on the first saturday of june.

16. Next monday is flag day.

17. My birthday is on july 10.

He, She, It, and *They* pages 136–137

Write a pronoun for the words in ( ).

18. (Summer vacation) is my favorite time.

19. (My brother and sister) are going to camp.

20. (My sister) went to camp last year.

21. (My brother) is going for the first time.

I and *Me* pages 138–139

Write the correct pronoun in ( ) to complete each sentence.

22. (I, me) stay home during the summer.

23. My mother finds things for (I, me) to do.

24. My friends and (I, me) play together.

Extra Practice

Adding *s* or *es* to Verbs   pages 172–173

Write the correct verb to finish each sentence.

1. I (walk, walks) in the woods with my class.

2. Our guide (teach, teaches) us about nature.

3. My friends and I (learn, learns) many things.

Combining Sentences with Verbs   pages 174–175

Use *and* to combine each pair of sentences. Write the new sentence.

4. We stop at the stream. We look for animals.

5. Adam spots a frog. Adam points to it.

Adding *ed* to Verbs   pages 182–183

Rewrite each sentence. Change the verb to tell about the past.

6. We <u>walk</u> along the stream.

7. I <u>point</u> at a turtle in the stream.

8. Everyone <u>looks</u> at the turtle.

Changing Verbs That End with *e*   pages 184–185

Write the verb in ( ) to tell about the past.

9. Adam (poke) at a rock in the water.

10. He (surprise) a crayfish.

Using *Am*, *Is*, and *Are* pages 200–201

Write *am*, *is*, or *are* to finish each sentence.

11. A crayfish _____ hard to find.

12. Turtles and frogs _____ easy to spot.

13. I _____ a good hiker.

Using *Was* and *Were* pages 202–203

Write *was* or *were* to finish each sentence.

14. We _____ hiking all day.

15. The animals _____ exciting to watch.

16. I _____ looking for a hawk.

17. Sam _____ watching for a raccoon.

Using *Has*, *Have*, and *Had* pages 210–211

Write *has*, *have*, or *had* to finish each sentence.

18. I _____ my backpack last time.

19. Adam _____ his backpack now.

20. Do you and your friends _____ places to hike?

21. We _____ to look for deer now.

Agreement with *Has*, *Have*, and *Had* pages 212–213

Write each sentence correctly.

22. Many parks <u>has</u> hiking trails.

23. Last year our park <u>have</u> one trail.

24. Now it <u>had</u> three hiking trails.

Extra Practice

Adjectives That Tell What Kind   pages 244–245

Choose an adjective from the box to complete each sentence. Write the sentence.

small	tall	round

1. The _____ pond is filled with water.

2. Two _____ goldfish swim in the pond.

3. A _____ plant pokes through the water.

Writing Longer Sentences   pages 246–247

Add adjectives to describe the underlined nouns in the sentences. Write each new sentence.

4. I see a <u>frog</u> on a <u>rock</u>.

5. A <u>turtle</u> is swimming in the <u>water</u>.

Adjectives for Taste, Smell, Feel, and Sound

pages 254–255

Choose an adjective from the box to complete each sentence. Write the sentence.

smooth	cool	gentle	wet

6. The water feels _____ and _____.

7. The frog has a _____ skin.

8. I hear the _____ sound of a waterfall.

Using Synonyms in Writing   pages 256–257

Choose the more exact adjective to finish each sentence.

9. A (soggy, wet) log rests by the pond.

10. A (large, huge) rock is in the water.

Adjectives That Tell How Many   pages 272–273

Write the adjective that tells how many.

11. I see three hawks in the sky.

12. Many birds are at the bird feeder.

13. There are two woodpeckers on the tree.

14. Several robins look for worms.

Using *a* and *an*   pages 274–275

Write *a* or *an* to complete each sentence.

15. I saw _____ owl in the forest.

16. It was sitting on the branch of _____ tree.

17. It did not move _____ feather.

18. Then it made _____ eerie hooting sound.

Adding *er* and *est*   pages 282–283

Write the correct form of the adjective in ( ) to finish each sentence.

19. A sparrow is (smaller, smallest) than an owl.

20. An ostrich is the (taller, tallest) bird of all.

21. A toucan's beak is (longer, longest) than my hand.

22. Parrots are the (smarter, smartest) birds of all.

Extra Practice

Using *Come*, *Run*, and *Give* pages 320–321

Write the correct verb in ( ) to complete each sentence.

1. Now Mom and Tina (come, came) home from shopping.

2. Let's (run, ran) outside to greet them.

3. Last month Dad (give, gave) us tickets for a play.

Joining Sentences pages 322–323

Use *and* to join the sentences. Remember to use a comma (,) before *and*.

4. I get ready to go. We all leave together.

5. We get into the car. Dad drives to the play.

6. Mom shows our tickets. We go into the theater.

Using *Go*, *Do*, and *See* pages 330–331

Write the correct verb in ( ) to complete each sentence.

7. We never (go, went) to the theater before last year.

8. Now we (see, saw) three plays each year.

9. We even (does, did) a children's play in school.

10. I hope we (do, did) another play soon!

Commas in Place Names and Dates   pages 332–333

Write the date and the name of the place correctly.

11. Mom saw a play in Chicago Illinois.

12. She will see another one on July 12 2002.

Using *Has*, *Have*, and *Had*   pages 348–349

Write the correct verb in ( ) to complete each sentence.

13. Dad (has, have) tickets to a movie museum.

14. Mom (had, has) a ticket last week.

15. Now we (has, have) one extra ticket.

Keeping to One Main Idea   pages 350–351

Write the paragraph. Underline the main idea. Leave out the sentence that does not tell about the main idea.

16.   Today we go to the movie museum. We will learn how movies are made. We will see some movies from the past. There is no school tomorrow. I want to learn about children in the movies.

Using Adverbs   pages 358–359

Write the adverb in each sentence. Then write *how*, *when*, or *where* for each adverb.

17. We arrived early in the morning.

18. We walked slowly into the museum.

19. People listened quietly to the person speaking.

20. I learned many things there.

Extra Practice

Noun-Pronoun Agreement pages 392–393

Write the pronoun that agrees with the underlined noun in each set of sentences.

1. The <u>children</u> get on the bus. _____ are excited.

2. The <u>bus</u> starts to move. _____ heads for the beach.

3. <u>Joe</u> can't wait. _____ wants to find a starfish.

4. <u>Liz</u> is excited, too. _____ wants to look for shells.

Word Order for Pronouns pages 394–395

Write the correct words in ( ) to complete each sentence.

5. Tim goes on a trip with (me and Liz, Liz and me).

6. (Liz and I, I and Liz) see the beach.

7. (The teacher and I, I and the teacher) get off the bus first.

Changing *y* to *i* pages 402–403

Write each verb in ( ) correctly.

8. Liz (hurry) to the shore.

9. Tim (carry) his camera to take pictures.

10. A seagull (fly) over our heads.

Writing Contractions   pages 404–405

Write the contraction for the underlined words.

11. Joe <u>has not</u> found a starfish.

12. Tim <u>is not</u> ready to take pictures yet.

Writing Longer Sentences   pages 420–421

Combine each set of sentences to make one longer sentence. Write the new sentence.

13. Boys swim. Girls swim.

14. Joe found a feather. Joe found a pretty shell.

Using a Series Comma   pages 422–423

Write each sentence correctly using the series commas.

15. Liz found an orange black and red shell.

16. Tim took a picture of Liz Joe Sam and me.

Using *there*, *their*, and *they're*   pages 430–431

Write *there*, *their*, or *they're* to complete each sentence.

17. Look at all the crabs over ____!

18. ____ running across the sand.

Using *to*, *too*, and *two*   pages 432–433

Write *to*, *too*, or *two* to complete each sentence.

19. We were at the beach for ____ hours.

20. Liz and Joe wanted ____ stay longer.

Handbook

Contents

Additional Writing Models

Writing Rubrics

Additional Writing Models

Invitation

In an **invitation**, a writer invites someone to come somewhere or to do something. An invitation has five parts.

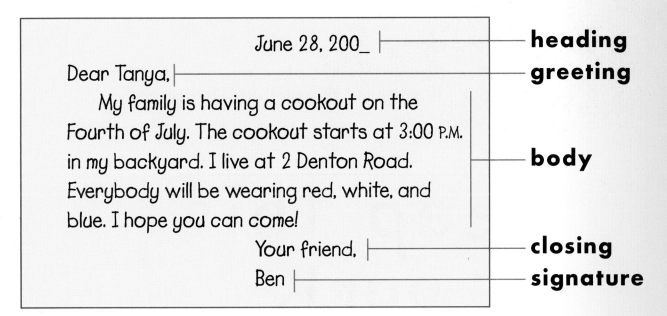

June 28, 200_ — **heading**

Dear Tanya, — **greeting**

My family is having a cookout on the Fourth of July. The cookout starts at 3:00 P.M. in my backyard. I live at 2 Denton Road. Everybody will be wearing red, white, and blue. I hope you can come! — **body**

Your friend, — **closing**

Ben — **signature**

An **envelope** is used to send a letter.

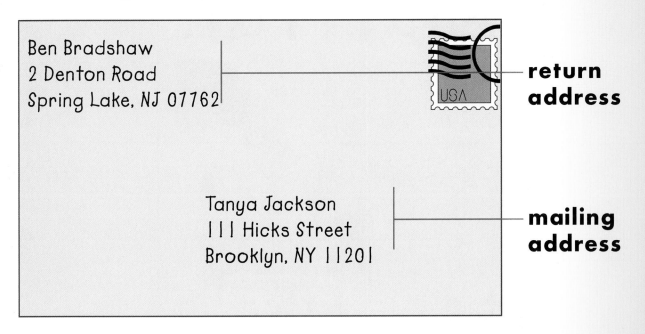

Ben Bradshaw
2 Denton Road
Spring Lake, NJ 07762 — **return address**

Tanya Jackson
111 Hicks Street
Brooklyn, NY 11201 — **mailing address**

Poster That Persuades

A **poster that persuades** shows how a problem can be solved. The writer draws a picture and writes words to show how the problem could be solved.

1 Decide on a topic. What is the problem? How could it be solved?

2 Draw a picture.

3 Write your ideas about the picture. Use some catchy words.

Play

In a **play**, a writer gives the setting, the characters' names, and what each character says.

1 Think of a title for your play. Write it at the top of the page.

2 Think about where the play takes place. This is the setting. Write the setting under the title.

3 Write each character's name at the beginning of a line.

4 Write what each character says. Think about how you talk with your friends and family members to help you.

The Ladybug Picnic

Setting: in a park

Characters: **Linda Ladybug, Larry Ladybug, and Lee Ladybug**

Linda: I hear that some people are having a picnic.

Larry: We should see what they brought.

Lee: I hope they have sandwiches.

Linda: Me, too. I love to eat the bread crumbs.

Larry: Let's go check out the picnic.

All Ladybugs: Yes! Let's go!

Writing Rubrics

How to Use Rubrics

The next six pages have checklists you can use to make your writing better. Each kind of writing has its own checklist. Here is how you can use them.

Before writing Look at the checklist to find out what your piece of writing should have.

During writing Check your draft against the list. Use the list to see how to make your writing better.

After writing Check your finished work against the list. Does your work show all the points?

Personal Story

Score of 4 ★★★★

★ My personal story tells about something that happened in my life. It uses words such as *I, me,* and *my.*

★ My personal story is complete and has a title.

★ My personal story uses time-order words to show the order in which things happened.

★ My personal story has few or no mistakes in punctuation, capitalization, or grammar.

Friendly Letter

Before writing Look at the checklist to find out what your letter should have.

During writing Check your draft against the list. Use the list to see how to make your writing better.

After writing Check your finished work against the list. Does your work show all the points?

Score of 4 ★★★★

- ★ My letter is written to someone I know. It tells the person about something I did.

- ★ My letter has all five parts. It has a heading, greeting, body, closing, and signature.

- ★ The body of my letter is clear. It has details that make it interesting to the reader.

- ★ My letter has few or no mistakes in punctuation, capitalization, or grammar.

Story

Before writing Look at the checklist to find out what your story should have.

During writing Check your draft against the list. Use the list to see how to make your writing better.

After writing Check your finished work against the list. Does your work show all the points?

Score of 4 ★★★★

★ My story is complete. It has a title and a beginning, middle, and ending.

★ My story has a problem that the story characters solve.

★ My story has exact words and details that help the reader understand the story events.

★ My story has few or no mistakes in punctuation, capitalization, or grammar.

Paragraph That Describes

Before writing Look at the checklist to find out what your paragraph that describes should have.

During writing Check your draft against the list. Use the list to see how to make your writing better.

After writing Check your finished work against the list. Does your work show all the points?

Score of 4 ★★★★

★ My paragraph that describes tells how something looks, sounds, smells, feels, or tastes.

★ My description has a topic sentence that tells what the paragraph is about. It has detail sentences that tell more about the topic.

★ My description uses details and colorful words that help the reader see what I am describing.

★ My description has few or no mistakes in punctuation, capitalization, or grammar.

How-to Paragraph

Before writing Look at the checklist to find out what your how-to paragraph should have.

During writing Check your draft against the list. Use the list to see how to make your writing better.

After writing Check your finished work against the list. Does your work show all the points?

Score of 4 ★★★★

★ My how-to paragraph is complete. It tells what the topic is, lists the materials first, and tells the steps to follow.

★ My how-to gives the steps in order. It uses time-order words to make the order clear.

★ My how-to has exact words and details that help the reader understand the steps.

★ My how-to has few or no mistakes in punctuation, capitalization, or grammar.

Research Report

Before writing Look at the checklist to find out what your research report should have.

During writing Check your draft against the list. Use the list to see how to make your writing better.

After writing Check your finished work against the list. Does your work show all the points?

Score of 4 ★★★★

- ★ My research report is about only one topic. Each main idea is stated in a sentence in a paragraph.

- ★ My report has details that help the reader understand the information.

- ★ My report is about something that is true. All the information is written in my own words.

- ★ My report has few or no mistakes in punctuation, capitalization, or grammar.

Spelling

Spelling Strategies

Here are five strategies that will help you spell many words.

1 If a word ends in a short vowel and a consonant, double the final consonant when you add an ending that begins with a vowel.

run + ing = running   **hop + ed = hopped**

2 If a word ends in *e*, drop the *e* when you add an ending that begins with a vowel.

make + ing = making   **race + ed = raced**

Keep the *e* when you add an ending that begins with a consonant.

nice + ly = nicely

3 If a word ends in a vowel and *y*, keep the *y* when you add an ending.

say + ing = saying   **gray + est = grayest**

4 If a word ends in a consonant and *y*, keep the *y* when adding *ing*.

cry + ing = crying

Change the *y* to *i* when you add other endings.

lady + es = ladies   **try + ed = tried**
funny + er = funnier

5 If a word ends in *s*, *x*, *ch*, or *sh*, add *es*.

bus + es = buses   **wash + es = washes**

Commonly Misspelled Words

again	it's	running
another	know	second
because	maybe	someone
better	might	their
broke(n)	missed	there
catch	off	third
caught	other	threw
children	people	too
didn't	please	trying
friend(s)	ready	were
happen(ed)	right	where

Manuscript Alphabet

Cursive Alphabet

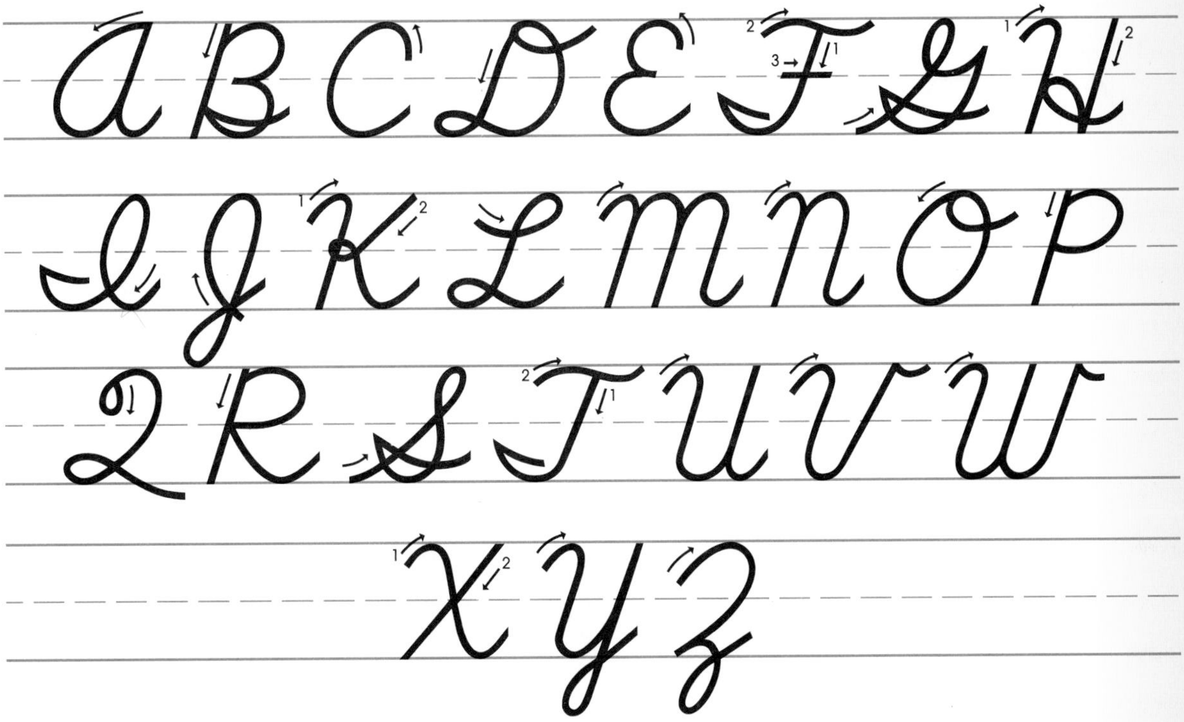

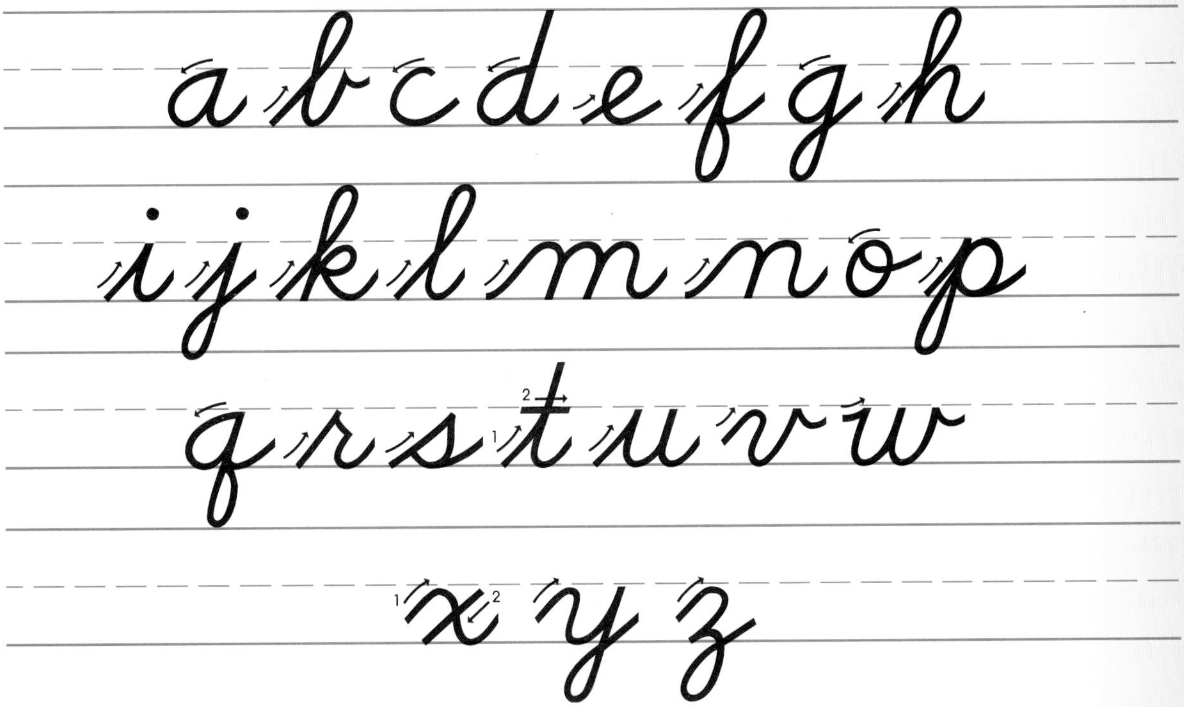

A B C D E F G H

I J K L M N O P

Q R S T U V W

X Y Z

a b c d e f g h

i j k l m n o p

q r s t u v w

x y z

D'Nealian Manuscript Alphabet

A B C D E F G H
I J K L M N O P
Q R S T U V W
X Y Z

a b c d e f g h
i j k l m n o p
q r s t u v w
x y z

Cursive Alphabet

$\mathcal{A}$ $\mathcal{B}$ $\mathcal{C}$ $\mathcal{D}$ $\mathcal{E}$ $\mathcal{F}$ $\mathcal{G}$ $\mathcal{H}$

$\mathcal{I}$ $\mathcal{J}$ $\mathcal{K}$ $\mathcal{L}$ $\mathcal{M}$ $\mathcal{N}$ $\mathcal{O}$ $\mathcal{P}$

$\mathcal{Q}$ $\mathcal{R}$ $\mathcal{S}$ $\mathcal{T}$ $\mathcal{U}$ $\mathcal{V}$ $\mathcal{W}$

$\mathcal{X}$ $\mathcal{Y}$ $\mathcal{Z}$

a b c d e f g h

i j k l m n o p

q r s t u v w

x y z

D'Nealian Manuscript Alphabet

A B C D E F G H
I J K L M N O P
Q R S T U V W
X Y Z

a b c d e f g h
i j k l m n o p
q r s t u v w
x y z

D'Nealian Cursive Alphabet

$$A\ B\ C\ D\ E\ F\ G\ H$$

$$I\ J\ K\ L\ M\ N\ O\ P$$

$$Q\ R\ S\ T\ U\ V\ W$$

$$X\ Y\ Z$$

$$a\ b\ c\ d\ e\ f\ g\ h$$

$$i\ j\ k\ l\ m\ n\ o\ p$$

$$q\ r\ s\ t\ u\ v\ w$$

$$x\ y\ z$$

Using a Thesaurus

Get to Know It! This **thesaurus** lists words and their **synonyms**. It also gives definitions and shows how a word is used in a sentence. The words in a thesaurus are in ABC order, or alphabetical order. Synonyms, which are words that have the same meaning, come after the example sentence. The opposites of most words are also listed.

Learn How to Use It! A good time to use the **thesaurus** is when you write and you are looking for a more interesting or more exact word. For example, find a better word for *big.* First find the *B* words and locate *big.* Then look at the list of **synonyms**, and pick the word that comes the closest to what you want to say. *Big* is on page 495.

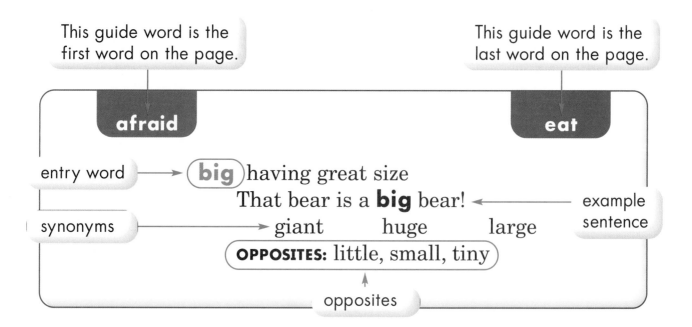

This guide word is the first word on the page.

This guide word is the last word on the page.

afraid

eat

entry word → (**big**) having great size

That bear is a **big** bear! ← example sentence

synonyms → giant   huge   large

OPPOSITES: little, small, tiny

opposites

A

afraid filled with fear
The mouse is **afraid** of the cat.
    frightened   scared
OPPOSITES: brave, fearless, unafraid

B

bad not good
The skunk has a **bad** smell.
    awful   dreadful   horrible   terrible
OPPOSITES: good, nice, pleasant, wonderful

big having great size
That bear is a **big** bear!
    giant   huge   large
OPPOSITES: little, small, tiny

C

cold having a low temperature
The weather is **cold** in the winter.
    chilly   cool   freezing   icy
OPPOSITES: hot, warm

cry to shed tears
Most babies **cry** when they are hungry.
    sob   wail   weep
OPPOSITES: chuckle, giggle, laugh

E

eat to take food into the body
I like to **eat** a snack after school.
    gobble   munch   nibble   taste

F

fat heavy; not skinny
We always have a **fat** turkey for Thanksgiving.
chubby   husky   plump   stout
OPPOSITES: skinny, slender, thin, trim

fun enjoyable
There were many **fun** rides at the park.
amusing   exciting
OPPOSITES: boring, dull

G

get to earn something
I hope I **get** an A on my test.
earn   obtain   receive
OPPOSITES: give, lose, send

go to move away from or toward a place
I **go** to the park on Saturdays.
hop   jump   race   ride
OPPOSITES: halt, remain, stay, stop

good pleasing or correct
That was a **good** movie.
fine   nice   pleasant

H

happy pleased
Sunny days make me feel **happy**.
cheerful   delighted   glad   merry
OPPOSITES: displeased, sad, unhappy

hard not easy
It is **hard** to learn a new sport.
difficult   tough
OPPOSITES: easy, simple

L

little not big in size
Kathy's doll was **little**.
short   small   tiny
OPPOSITES: big, huge, large, tall

M

make to cause something to happen
The workers **make** a house.
build   create   shape

N

nice pleasant or good
We go to the park when it is **nice** outside.
beautiful   kind   lovely
OPPOSITES: awful, bad, mean, unpleasant

P

pretty nice-looking
Janet wore a **pretty** dress.
beautiful   lovely
OPPOSITES: ordinary, plain, ugly

R

run to move quickly
I **run** after my brother.
dash   hurry   race

sad unhappy
Michael was **sad** when he lost his hat.
blue   gloomy   miserable   sorry
OPPOSITES: cheerful, glad, happy

see to use your eyes to look at something
We **see** animals at the zoo.
notice   stare   watch

take to move or carry something
Take your toys upstairs.
carry   get   move

walk to move by using the feet
Ana and Carlos **walk** to the store.
step   stroll

well in a good or correct way
My sister plays sports **well**.
easily   skillfully
OPPOSITES: badly, poorly

Glossary

Using the Glossary

Get to Know It! The **glossary** gives the meanings of grammar and writing terms that are highlighted in *Harcourt Language*. It also gives sentences that have examples of the terms. The words in the **glossary** are in ABC order, or **alphabetical order**.

Learn How to Use It! If you want to find the word *exclamation* in the **glossary**, you should first find the *E* words. *E* is near the beginning of the alphabet, so the *E* words are near the beginning of the **glossary**. Then you can use the guide words at the top of the page to help you find the entry word *exclamation*.

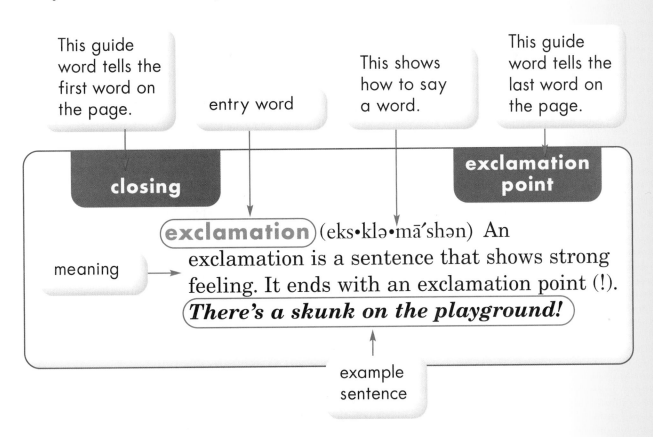

This guide word tells the first word on the page.

entry word

This shows how to say a word.

This guide word tells the last word on the page.

closing

exclamation point

meaning

(exclamation) (eks•klə•mā′shən) An exclamation is a sentence that shows strong feeling. It ends with an exclamation point (!). *There's a skunk on the playground!*

example sentence

A

abbreviation (ə·brē·vē·ā′shən) An abbreviation is a short way of writing a word. **Mr. Johnson went to work.**

adjective (aj′ik·tiv) A word that tells about a noun. An adjective can compare or tell how many or what kind. **I have *three* sisters.**

adverb (ad′vûrb) An adverb tells about a verb. An adverb can tell when, where, or how. **My team played baseball *yesterday*.**

antonym (an′tə·nim) A word that has an opposite meaning of another word is an antonym. ***Plain* and *fancy* are antonyms.**

apostrophe (ə·pos′trə·fē) An apostrophe (') takes the place of missing letters in a contraction or shows possession in a possessive noun. ***Molly's* sister *can't* come today.**

atlas (at′ləs) An atlas is a book of maps. **Use the atlas to see where India is.**

B

body (bod′ē) The body of a letter is the friendly message. **Write about your trip in the body of your letter.**

C

characters (kar′ək·tərz) The people or animals in a story are the characters. **Who are the main characters in this story?**

closing (klō′zing) The closing of a letter is the part that says good-bye. **Maria ended her letter by writing the closing** *Your friend.*

command (kə·mand′) A command is a sentence that tells someone to do something. ***Please close the door.***

contraction (kən·trak′shən) A contraction is a short way to write two words. **I** *can't* **wait for you to come!**

details (dē·tālz′) Details are examples that help explain a main idea. **Tony added details to make his report interesting.**

draft (draft) A first try at writing something is a draft. **Pam made changes to the first draft of her story.**

exclamation (eks·klə·mā′shən) An exclamation is a sentence that shows strong feeling. It ends with an exclamation point (!). ***There's a skunk on the playground!***

exclamation point (eks·klə·mā′shən point) An exclamation point (!) at the end of a sentence shows strong feeling. **Look out for that ball***!*

fiction books (fik′shən books) Fiction books are made-up stories. **I read a fiction book about going to Jupiter.**

greeting (grēt′ing) The greeting of a letter is the part that says hello. **The greeting of Beth's letter was *Dear Grandpa*.**

heading (hed′ing) The heading of a letter tells the date and the writer's address. **Put the date in the heading of your letter.**

helping verb (help′ing vûrb) A helping verb works with the main verb to tell about an action. **I *have* learned about plants.**

homophones (hom′ə·fōnz) Words that sound alike but have different meanings are homophones. ***Pear* and *pair* are homophones.**

how-to paragraph (hou tōō′ par′ə·graf) A how-to paragraph is one in which a writer tells how to make or do something. **Ying told how to bake cookies in her how-to paragraph.**

main idea (mān i·dē′ə) The main idea is the most important idea in a paragraph. **What is the main idea of Adolfo's paragraph?**

naming part (nām′ing pärt) The naming part of a sentence tells who or what the sentence is about. *Frances* **went to the movies.**

noun (noun) A noun is a word that names a person, place, animal, or thing. **The *boy* brought his *ball* to the *park*.**

nonfiction books (non·fik′shən bŏoks) Nonfiction books tell about things that are real. **Janie read a nonfiction book about snakes.**

outline (out′līn) An outline shows the order of main ideas and details in a piece of writing. **Check your outline for all the parts of your report.**

paragraph (par′ə·graf) A group of sentences that all tell about a main idea is a paragraph. **Mikey's paragraph is about dogs.**

period (pir′ē·əd) Use a period (.) at the end of a statement or a command. **I saw the monkeys.**

possessive noun (pə·zes′iv noun) A noun that shows ownership. ***Pablo's* book is on the *teacher's* desk.**

pronoun (prō′noun) A word that takes the place of a noun is a pronoun. ***I* played soccer, and *he* watched.**

proper noun (prop′ər noun) A noun that tells the special name of a person, a place, or an animal is a proper noun. It begins with a capital letter. ***Hector* lives in *New York*.**

Q

question (kwes′chən) A question is a sentence that asks something. It ends with a question mark (?). ***Where is my other shoe?***

question mark (kwes′chən märk) Use a question mark (?) at the end of a question. **Do you like to play soccer?**

S

sentence (sen′təns) A sentence is a group of words that tells a complete thought. Every sentence begins with a capital letter and ends with an end mark. ***The children ride the bus to school.***

setting (set′ing) The setting is where and when a story takes place. **The setting of the story is long ago in the woods.**

signature (sig′nə·chər) The signature of a letter is the writer's handwritten name at the end. **I wrote my signature at the end of my letter.**

statement (stāt′mənt) A statement is a sentence that tells something. It ends with a period (.). *I like grape juice.*

synonym (sin′ə·nim) A word that means the same or almost the same as another word. **Beautiful is a synonym for *pretty*.**

telling part (tel′ing pärt) The telling part of a sentence tells what someone or something is or does. **Jasmine *walks her dog*.**

thesaurus (thə·sôr′əs) A thesaurus lists words in alphabetical order and gives synonyms for each word. **Look up the word in the thesaurus to find words with the same or almost the same meaning.**

verb (vûrb) A verb is a word that tells what someone or something is or does. **The frog *jumps* from spot to spot.**

Vocabulary Power

angrily My brother slammed the door **angrily**.

ambassador Mrs. Ruiz is an **ambassador** of Mexico.

burrow The rabbits **burrow** underground.

cocoons Caterpillars turn into moths in their **cocoons**.

considerate It was **considerate** of you to clean my room.

consulting He was **consulting** the teacher about what to do.

contribution Her **contribution** made the class better.

correspondence They had a written **correspondence**.

countryside The **countryside** has many trees.

creatures Different **creatures** live in the rain forest.

croak The frogs in the pond **croak** loudly.

demonstrate Marcy will **demonstrate** how to bake a cake.

dignified The mayor looked important and **dignified**.

explored My cousin and I **explored** my attic.

fastened She **fastened** the baby's jacket.

flutter They saw the baby bird **flutter** its wings.

glossiest My book has the **glossiest** cover.

guided The leader **guided** his tour group.

harmony The singers sang in perfect **harmony**.

infinite The universe seems **infinite**.

international The singer is an **international** success.

lullaby Grandma sang me a **lullaby** every night.

luscious I ate a tasty, **luscious** peach yesterday.

marvelous We had a **marvelous** time at the party!

mockingbird I saw a **mockingbird** in the tree.

quicker The cheetah is **quicker** than a lion.

ragged The worn-out old doll wore a **ragged** coat.

rattlesnake A **rattlesnake** is very poisonous.

recycled We **recycled** all of our old newspapers.

revolving My sister got stuck in a **revolving** door!

rodeo My uncle rides bulls at the **rodeo**.

scamper The mice **scamper** into their hole.

seize Will the player **seize** the ball?

species Are whales an endangered **species**?

whirl Watch the dancers **whirl** and twirl!

wholly It is **wholly** likely that the team will lose.

Index

U

Usage. *See also* Grammar; Punctuation

V

W

Acknowledgments

For permission to reprint copyrighted material, grateful acknowledgment is made to the following sources:

Atheneum Books for Young Readers, an imprint of Simon & Schuster Children's Publishing Division: "August Afternoon" from *Open the Door* by Marion Edey and Dorothy Grider. Published by Charles Scribner's Sons, NY, 1949. From *Jalapeño Bagels* by Natasha Wing, illustrated by Robert Casilla. Text copyright © 1996 by Natasha Wing; illustrations copyright © 1996 by Robert Casilla.

Candlewick Press, Cambridge, MA: "Who's Been Sleeping in My Porridge?" and illustration from *Who's Been Sleeping in My Porridge?* by Colin McNaughton. Copyright © 1990 by Colin McNaughton.

Creative Type, Arcata, CA, www.losbagels.com: Recipe for "Jalapeño Bagels" from *Los Bagels Recipes & Lore.* Copyright © 1991 by Los Bagels.

Dial Books for Young Readers, a division of Penguin Putnam Inc.: Cover illustration by Leo and Diane Dillon from *Why Mosquitoes Buzz in People's Ears* by Verna Aardema. Illustration copyright © 1975 by Leo and Diane Dillon. From *Red Riding Hood* by James Marshall. Copyright © 1987 by James Marshall.

Phyllis Halloran: "Busy" by Phyllis Halloran. Text copyright © 1989 by Phyllis Halloran.

Harcourt, Inc.: "Little Silk Worms" from *Dragon Kites and Dragonflies* by Demi Hitz. Copyright © 1986 by Demi. Cover illustration from *Check It Out! The Book About Libraries* by Gail Gibbons. Copyright © 1985 by Gail Gibbons. "Giraffes" from *The Llama Who Had No Pajama: 100 Favorite Poems* by Mary Ann Hoberman. Text copyright © 1973 by Mary Ann Hoberman. Cover illustration by Ted Rand from *Willie Takes a Hike* by Gloria Rand. Illustration copyright © 1996 by Ted Rand.

HarperCollins Publishers: Cover illustration from *How a Book Is Made* by Aliki. Copyright © 1986 by Aliki Brandenberg. "Tommy" from *Bronzeville Boys and Girls* by Gwendolyn Brooks. Text copyright © 1956 by Gwendolyn Brooks Blakely. Cover illustration from *Feel the Wind* by Arthur Dorros. Copyright © 1989 by Arthur Dorros. From *You're Aboard Spaceship Earth* by Patricia Lauber, illustrated by Holly Keller. Text copyright © 1996 by Patricia G. Lauber; illustrations copyright © 1996 by Holly Keller. From *Red Dancing Shoes* by Denise Lewis Patrick, illustrated by James E. Ransome. Text copyright © 1993 by Denise Lewis Patrick; illustrations copyright © 1993 by James E. Ransome. "I Am Running in a Circle" from *New Kid on the Block* by Jack Prelutsky. Text copyright © 1984 by Jack Prelutsky. "Something Big Has Been Here" from *Something Big Has Been Here* by Jack Prelutsky. Text copyright © 1990 by Jack Prelutsky. Cover illustration from *The Acorn Tree and Other Folktales*, retold and illustrated by Anne Rockwell. Copyright © 1995 by Anne Rockwell. Cover illustration by Steven Kellogg from *If You Made a Million* by David M. Schwartz. Illustration copyright © 1989 by Steven Kellogg.

Elizabeth Hauser: "Spring Rain" from *Around and About* by Marchette Chute. Text copyright 1957 by E. P. Dutton; text copyright renewed 1985 by Marchette Chute.

Holiday House, Inc.: From *Penguins!* by Gail Gibbons. Copyright © 1998 by Gail Gibbons. Cover illustration from *Weather Words and What They Mean* by Gail Gibbons. Copyright © 1990 by Gail Gibbons. Cover illustration from *Who's Who in My Family?* by Loreen Leedy. Copyright © 1995 by Loreen Leedy.

Houghton Mifflin Company: Cover illustration by Blair Lent from *Why the Sun and the Moon Live in the Sky* by Elphinstone Dayrell. Copyright © 1968 by Blair Lent, Jr. "The Flying Machine" from *George and Martha* by James Marshall. Copyright © 1972 by James Marshall.

Ideals Children's Books, Nashville, Tennessee: From *Don't Forget to Write* by Martina Selway. Copyright © 1992 by Martina Selway.

Hettie Jones: Untitled poem (retitled: "The Mockingbird") by Acoma from *The Trees Stand Shining: Poetry of the North American Indians* by Hettie Jones. Text copyright © 1971 by Hettie Jones.

Alfred A. Knopf, a Division of Random House Inc.: "April Rain Song" by Langston Hughes from *Collected Poems* by Langston Hughes. Text copyright © 1994 by the Estate of Langston Hughes.

Lee & Low Books, Inc., 95 Madison Avenue, New York, NY 10016: "Sun Song" from *Confetti: Poems for Children* by Pat Mora, illustrated by Enrique O. Sanchez. Text copyright © 1996 by Pat Mora; illustration copyright © 1996 by Enrique O. Sanchez.

Little, Brown and Company (Inc.): "This Is My Rock" from *Far and Few* by David McCord. Text copyright 1929 by David McCord. Originally published in *The Saturday Review.*

Margaret K. McElderry Books, an imprint of Simon & Schuster Children's Publishing Division: From *Dear Mr. Blueberry* by Simon James. Copyright © 1991 by Simon James.

Pearson Education: Cover illustration by Randy Verougstraete from *A Money Adventure: Earning, Saving, Spending, Sharing* by Neale S. Godfrey. Copyright © 1996 by Children's Financial Network, Inc. Published by Modern Curriculum Press.

Philomel Books, a division of Penguin Putnam Inc.: Illustration by Eric Carle from *Animals Animals*, edited by Laura Whipple. Illustration copyright © 1989 by Eric Carle. "There's a Cow on the Mountain" (retitled: "The Cow") and illustration by Ed Young from *Chinese Mother Goose Rhymes*, selected and edited by Robert Wyndham. Text copyright © 1968 by Robert Wyndham; illustration copyright © 1968 by Ed Young.

G. P. Putnam's Sons, a division of Penguin Putnam Inc.: Cover illustration from *Officer Buckle and Gloria* by Peggy Rathmann. Copyright © 1995 by Peggy Rathmann.

Marian Reiner: "Hurry" from *Out Loud* by Eve Merriam. Text copyright © 1973 by Eve Merriam. "On Our Way" from *Catch a Little Rhyme* by Eve Merriam. Text copyright © 1966 by Eve Merriam; text © renewed 1994 by Dee Michel and Guy Michel.

Scholastic Inc.: From *Fire Fighters* by Robert Maass. Copyright © 1989 by Robert Maass.

Simon & Schuster Books for Young Readers, an imprint of Simon & Schuster Children's Publishing Division: From *Kate Heads West* by Pat Brisson, illustrated by Rick Brown. Text copyright © 1990 by Pat Brisson; illustrations copyright © 1990 by Rick Brown. From *Two Greedy Bears* by Mirra Ginsburg, illustrated by Jose Aruego and Ariane Dewey. Text copyright © 1976 by Mirra Ginsburg; illustrations copyright © 1976 by Jose Aruego and Ariane Dewey. From *I Have a Pet!* by Shari Halpern. Copyright © 1994 by Shari Halpern. Cover illustration by Diane Greenseid from *Wilson Sat Alone* by Debra Hess. Illustration copyright © 1994 by Diane Greenseid.

United Indians of All Tribes Foundation: "The Wind is Cool and Swift" by Tanu Frank from *Daybreak Star Indian Reader.*

Photo Credits

Unit One:
Pages 22-23: Ken Kenzie/Harcourt.

Unit Two:
Pages 94-95: Index Stock Photography.

Unit Three:
Pages 168-169: Harcourt.

Unit Four:
Pages 240-241: Steve Terrill/The Stock Market NY.

Unit Five:
Pages 316-317: Harcourt;
FireFighters photos, pages 338-339: Robert Maass.

Unit 6:
Pages 388-389: Michael Yamashita/Woodfin Camp & Associates.

Other photos: Harcourt.

Illustration Credits

Andrea Tachiera pp. 24, 25; Marsha Winborn pp. 36, 38, 39, 40, 41, 42, 43, 96, 96, 134, 135, 318, 356, 357, 358, 359, 360, 361, 362, 365; Margeaux Lucas pp. 46, 47, 48, 53, 81, 193, 194, 195, 196, 261, 280, 281, 282, 284, 285, 288, 302, 305, 306, 319, 330, 331, 334, 336, 375, 377, 378, 379, 380, 383, 420, 422, 423, 424, 427, 443; Deirdre Newman pp. 52, 58, 105, 131, 141, 337, 409; Alexi Natchev pp. 54, 55, 56, 57, 58, 60, 244, 245, 246, 247, 248, 249, 250; Benton Mahan pp. 63, 64, 65, 66, 67, 68, 70, 208, 209, 346, 347, 348, 349, 350, 351, 352, 353, 354; Dave Winter pp. 71, 198, 199, 271, 272, 273, 274, 275, 276, 278, 418; Myron Grossman pp. 106, 107, 110, 112, 137, 140, 142; Randy Chewning pp. 124, 125, 126, 127, 128, 129, 130, 132, 200, 202, 203, 204, 205, 206, 228, 229, 230, 231, 232, 234, 235, 265, 266, 267, 435, 436, 438, 448, 450; Janet Broxen pp. 208, 209, 270; Laura Huliska-Beith pp. 210, 211, 254, 255, 256, 257, 258, 260, 328, 329, 401, 402, 403, 404, 405, 406, 408; Dawn Appelby pp. 320, 321, 322, 323, 324, 326; Ande Cook pp. 390, 391; George Thompson pp. 392, 393, 394, 395, 396, 398; Bart Rivers pp. 428, 429, 430, 432, 434, 436; Ethan Long p. 481